JAMAICA FAREWELL

JAMAICA FAREWELL

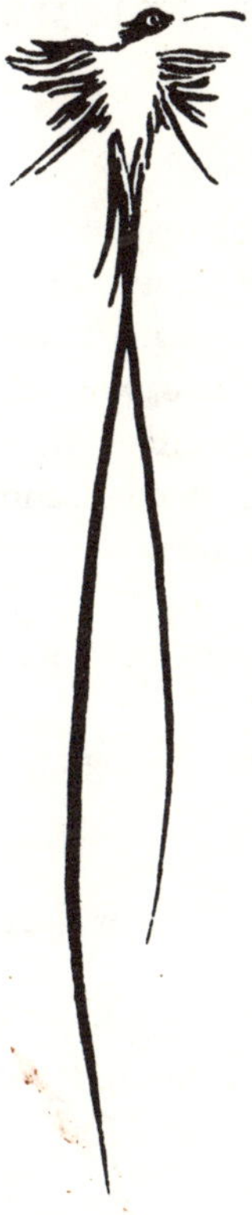

by
Morris Cargill

BARRICADE BOOKS • NEW YORK

Published by Barricade Books Inc.
150 Fifth Avenue
New York, NY 10011

Printed in the United States of America.

Library of Congress Cataloging-in-Publication Data

Cargill, Morris.
Jamaica farewell / Morris Cargill.
p. cm.
ISBN 1-56980-031-6 (pbk.): $7.95
1. Jamaica—Social life and customs. 2. Plantation life—Jamaica. 3. Cargill, Morris. I. Title.
F1874.C37 1995
972.92'05'092—dc20 94-45638
CIP

First printing

To
Patricia Elaine

1

The garden at Charlottenburgh overlooks a valley. On the far side of the valley are some low hills. Behind those are the Blue Mountains, and behind them again is Blue Mountain Peak. Three carrion crows, a kind of turkey-buzzard known locally as John Crow, glide and circle above the valley with their black wings flapping occasionally to overcome an unexpected down-current of air. A slight wind rustles the leaves of the almond tree which presently shades me from the afternoon sun.

Twenty-seven years ago, my first wife, Barbara, and I planted that tree as we had planted nearly every other tree on

Charlottenburgh. She had laid out the garden on land that had once been a canefield, and we had put in pine trees, a bay tree, and peach trees, planted mangos, lychees, limes, lemons, oranges, cherries, guavas, star-apples and figs, among others. Vanilla and black-pepper vines grew up into the ackee trees, and wild orchids grew in profusion.

Barbara had established nearly five hundred different kinds of plants and flowers on our three acres of garden with not very much help from the assorted nongardeners we had employed. Finally, a young Indian called Claudius Doolam, to whom gardening was a vocation, had come along. Between them, after the hurricane of 1951, they had made the garden into a place of tranquility and beauty.

From where I sit under the almond tree, I can see old Tom McIntosh approaching. Tom is as near jet-black as it is possible for anyone to be. But in the last national census he put himself down as Scottish, which is one of about a million reasons why censuses in Jamaica are works of fiction. Jamaicans use words for therapeutic reasons rather than for communication. They will always try to give the answer they think will please you or to arrange words in the manner which they themselves find pleasant or reassuring. Facts are not of great importance.

Old Tom likes to think of himself as a Scotsman though he does not, I know, have the faintest idea where Scotland is. Neither he nor anyone else knows how old he is, though I would guess he is not far off eighty.

About five years ago, I thought it was time that his days of serious work should come to an end, though he appeared active and strong. My farm manager gave him a hammer and a supply of staples and a new job to tour the fences of the estate and mend any gaps in them. It took him about three months to make a complete circuit of the boundary, and then he would start all over again. It was mild exercise, kept him out in the open, and gave him a sense of purpose. Any serious damage to the fences, including, on occasion, damage done by Tom's efforts, was mended by an expert fenceman.

As old Tom comes nearer, I see that tears are running down his cheeks, glistening in the afternoon sun. I get up in some alarm and ask him what is the matter. I suspect that getting the answer will take a bit of time, since one pursues facts in Jamaica in a roundabout manner, for facts are dangerous and alien things and must be approached warily.

"It's that nasty, dirty-mouth girl, Lurleen," says Tom.

"What about her?"

"I am in de field, Boss, minding my own business and mending de fence–Lurleen is a dirty girl."

More tears flow down Tom's cheeks, and I wait patiently for him to recover.

"May de Lawd bring punishment down upon her head," Tom adds after a pause.

"Right, Tom," says I. "But what did she do to you?"

"I am in de field, Boss, working carefuly upon de fence. And it is true that I see de cow June in de field. June is a bad cow, Boss. She like to eat green bananas."

"Then what happened?" I prompted.

"When I come out of de field to Roadside Gate, Boss, Lurleen is standing in de road. She talking to some idlers and saying things I don't like to hear."

"What was she saying?"

"Begging your pardon, Boss. I have to say some things to you I should not say."

"Don't mind me," I reassured him. "Just get on with it."

"You know what dat nasty, dirty-mouth girl is saying to dem idlers, Boss? Begging your pardon, sir. She say she see me in de field a fuck your cow, June."

"That is a wicked thing for her to say, Tom," I observe.

"It is very wicked. And you know what hurt me, Boss? Lurleen know I would never do a thing like that to you. I am a faithful worker. I know you send de milk to de Condensary. And I know dey don't like to take milk from cows what have sexual intercourse with humans."

Even if I wish to call Tom's morals into question, I do not dream of doubting the logic of his loyalty. So I comfort him, promising action against Lurleen. And when he leaves, somewhat consoled, I take a run down to the dairy in my small jeep to have a word with Abdul Edoo, the head cattleman.

The bush telegraph, which seems to operate at a speed faster than light, has already informed Abdul about Lurleen's accusations.

"You come 'bout ole Tom, Bossy?" he asks, cackling with glee.

"Yes."

"It is not true, you hear, Bossy."

The word "bossy" is an intimate form of the word "boss," and it is used only in special circumstances by employees in the country parts of Jamaica. Old Tom calls me "bossy," too. But the intimate form is dropped when something of great seriousness has to be discussed. I am called various things by the people on Charlottenburgh. "Honey Boy" is preferred by the older women; "Squire" by the older men; "Sahib" by most of the Indians. And, for some reason or another, "Manager" by the ranger. But most of them also use the term "bossy" when they're feeling charitable towards me.

Forms of address can be complicated. When my second wife arrived at Charlottenburgh, she was regarded as a stranger to be kept at arm's length and was addressed as Mrs. Cargill. When, within quite a short time, people began calling her "Miss Pat," I knew she had been accepted.

"How do you know it's not true, Abdul?" I asked.

"Because it would take at least two men to hold dat cow."

So now I shall have to do something about Lurleen. But what?

I drive back home and sit again under my almond tree to

think about it and to think about something else that has been troubling me for some time. It is a painful thing to think about. There is the possibility that I may have to leave Charlottenburgh and Jamaica. My roots are deep here, and there are so many pleasures, memories, obligations.

2

Owning and running a plantation in Jamaica is not just a matter of farm organization. It is also a mixture of running an institution for delinquents and operating a system of social services. Add to this the need to know how to function as a kind of medical orderly, a legal advisor, and a public amanuensis. There are also many situations in which it is essential to stretch, even to break, the law.

Take, for instance, the case of Miss Mumma. Miss Mumma, her man, two young sons and a daughter, all arrived on the plantation fifteen years ago looking for work. I assigned them a cottage. The man died six months later. Miss

Mumma stayed on. She was a pleasant woman and a good worker. She had not been with me for a year, however, before she went off her head, shouting, laughing, and rushing up and down the road in sustained manic excitement. With great difficulty I got her into the back of my car, with two men to hold her still, and took her to the doctor.

After he had observed her a while, he said, "I'm afraid I can't help you with this one. I am not a psychiatrist. And she is suffering from some kind of psychosis. The best thing for her would be to get her into the mental hospital in Kingston where she can get proper treatment."

"Can you arrange to have her admitted?" I asked.

"No. Unfortunately. The District Medical Officer will have to certify her."

"Well, I'll take her to him now."

"You haven't heard me out yet, my friend," the doctor said. "The only way you can get the DMO to certify her insane is to have the police make the application. And the only way the police will make the application is for you to have them arrest her and put her in the lockup."

"But that is insane!" I said.

"Well, the mental hospital can't hold all our legislators, you know. You'll just have to figure out some way to have her arrested. Sorry I can't be of more help. In the meantime, I will give her a sedative."

So I drove to the police station in our little village of Highgate, and asked to see the corporal on duty. The corporal's interest in me and, indeed, in anything else apart from his fingernails, which he was busy poking at with an old steel nailfile, was minimal.

"I have a woman on my farm who has gone off her head," I said. "And I would like to have her committed to Bellevue."

"I can't send her to Bellevue," he said, hardly looking up from his cuticle control.

"I know you can't," I persisted. "But if you arrest her, maybe the DMO will."

"It's Friday now. We are not going to get no DMO till Monday. He has gone fishing." The corporal paused, then added, "Anyway, I can't arrest her if she's not going on bad."

"What do you call going on bad?" I asked warily.

The corporal frowned and once more reluctantly tore his attention away from his fingernails. "Well, just going on bad 'n' like. We pick up a man last week who take off all him clothes and was walking naked along the street—a madman."

"This woman," I said firmly, "is going on very bad."

"How she so quiet in the back of the car then?"

I had clearly underrated this corporal. He had been observing more than his fingernails.

"She was given a sedative," I told him.

"You take her back to the farm, and I come dis evening."

I was glad of the delay. It would give me time to organize some "going on bad" on the part of poor Miss Mumma.

We didn't have to do much organizing. By the time we got Miss Mumma back to her cottage, the sedative had worn off, and she was raising hell. She leapt out of the car, pulled herself free from the ranger's restraining hand, and started to march up and down the road at a great speed singing a hymn at the top of her voice. We just let her get on with it, not knowing what else to do. In between each verse of the hymn, which was "Onward Christian Soldiers," she would pause and laugh in a high-pitched way, then she would start to sing again.

So we left her, and I told the ranger I would be back later.

That evening I returned before dark with the farm manager and the headman. Miss Mumma was still walking about, still singing. When she saw us, she shouted, "Dey's coming for me, but de Lawd will protect me!" Then she began another round of "Onward Christian Soldiers."

But she was harming nobody; not even herself. If singing hymns out of tune in a manic sort of way was an example of "going on bad," then half the congregations of our churches would be in jail.

I explained the problem to the farm manager and to the headman. They thought about it for a while and then the headman, a most resourceful man, said, "If she broke de window, dat would be 'going on bad.' "

It sounded a good idea, but costly.

"Well, then. One windowpane only," I pleaded, "and wait until the corporal arrives."

We had not long to wait. Miss Mumma's cottage, about fifty yards from the road, was reached by a path through the banana walk. When we heard the engine of the police jeep in the distance coming down the hill, the farm manager and the headman grabbed Miss Mumma and practically carried her down the path to the front of her cottage. Within a few moments, we could see through the trees that the police jeep had arrived. It stopped, and two policemen got out. They started to walk down the pathway.

At which point there was a tremendous crash. An entire window of Miss Mumma's cottage had been shattered. The headman was grinning happily. "Might as well it look good," he observed. The two policemen came on the run.

"What's that noise?" asked one of them, a constable, drawing his revolver. The other was the corporal to whom we had spoken.

"Is all right, Corpy," said the headman. "It's only Miss Mumma shy a rock through de window."

The alleged perpetrator of this wicked deed was, in the meantime, still walking up and down with great speed, but the hymn had now changed to "Glory, Glory, Hallelujah."

"She's off her head," said the ranger, who had just reappeared upon the scene.

"She going to do herself harm," said the farm manager.

"She going on bad?" asked the constable.

"She going on very bad," replied the headman.

Miss Mumma gave no trouble as the two policemen held her arms and led her down the path toward the jeep. As she passed me, she looked at me, paused in her singing, and observed: "Lord, I have been betrayed by a Judas."

You can't fool a mad person.

3

Miss Mumma was kept in the police lockup in our village for two days before the DMO certified her and had her admitted to the mental hospital in Kingston.

That was the beginning of a series of problems concerning Miss Mumma, which led me into breaking the law in ways more serious than merely framing her. Getting Miss Mumma locked up and certified became a routine. On this occasion she remained in the mental hospital for three months and returned to Charlottenburgh in sound mental health. She would have such remissions for a year; sometimes longer. Then she would go off, and we would have to have her arrested all over again. In ten years we must have repeated the process five times.

In the early stages of this process, I got some help from an unexpected quarter. Soon after her return from Bellevue on the first occasion, a wild-looking man arrived on the plantation asking for work. He was a member of a sect known as the Ras Tafarians and he was what was known as a locksman. He had grown his hair into long, scraggly curls which hung down to his shoulders and partly covered his face.

The Ras Tafarians are a strange sect that regard Haile Selassie of Ethiopia as a god. Even now they do not believe that Haile Selassie is dead. When, sometime ago, His Imperial Majesty Haile Selassie I–Power of the Holy Trinity, 225th Emperor of the 3,000-year-old Ethiopian Empire, Elect of God, Lord of Lords, King of Kings, Heir to the Throne of Solomon, Conquering Lion of Judah–arrived by air on an official visit to Jamaica, he was amazed to find that he had been deified by the Ras Tafarians of Jamaica in 1930, on his ascension to the throne of Ethiopia. They were the first Jamaicans he saw upon arrival, for they had mobbed the airport, broken through the cordons of soldiers and police and had surrounded the aircraft, smoking tobacco and pot, so that the slightest gasoline leak would have blown them and their god to Kingdom Come.

No living deity has ever been so terrified by his worshippers. During his brief stay, the Emperor of Ethiopia kept them at a safe distance, but this in no way lessened his followers' religious zeal.

It is difficult to say what the Ras Tafarians believe in. Their replies to questions are a jumble of irrational and muddled thoughts and quasi-theological non sequiturs. But I suppose the nearest translation of their assorted incoherencies is that they regard themselves as black Hebrews exiled in a world called Babylon, worshipping a black god. White men, they say, have been worshipping a dead god and have been trying to teach black men to do likewise. They believe that the King James version of the Bible is a distortion of the truth; that the black race was punished by God with slavery for sinning. To them Ethiopia is Zion, to which, their sins forgiven, they will eventually return.

The Ras Tafarians don't eat pork or drink alcohol, but marijuana is to them the Holy Herb, though its use is illegal in Jamaica. They do not vote and do not like to be permanently employed. The best-known Ras Tafarian today is Bob Marley, the reggae millionaire, to whom the tax haven of Nassau has become a rather more practical Zion than Ethiopia.

Behind all the Ras Tafarian fundamentalist gobbledegook is, nevertheless, a sound psychological truth. In the twenties in Jamaica, the black man had only two courses open to him if he wished to try to save a self-respect cruelly assailed on all sides by the lunatic irrationality of color prejudice. He could on the one hand try to work himself up in the world and to become a kind of "Black Englishman." Many had tried this with unhappy results. Or he could simply drop out of the society which insulted him, developing a religion, a culture and a way of life which, by totally excluding the white man and all his works, put him beyond the reach of white snubs and prejudiced white value judgments. Any rationale which suited his purpose would have "worked" so long as it was within the reach and within the understanding of the uneducated and limited people involved.

At a certain level the Ras Tafarian way was the better. The Rastas preached love, peace and reconciliation between people and races. Freed from the daily impact of white-supremacy doctrines, they gained self-confidence and shed the chips-on-the-shoulder with which more "respectable" Blacks were constantly burdened. The genuine Ras Tafarians are people in their own right, which makes them pleasant and easy to meet in spite of their forbidding appearance and theological inanities. Come to that, the same thing could be said about a surprising number of other religious sects.

The trouble is, however, to tell the genuine Ras Tafarian from the assorted criminals who soon found that it was relatively easy to avoid the police by growing their hair and getting lost among the Ras Tafarian settlements. This criminal element soon got the Ras Tafarians, and especially the locksmen or "Dreads," in bad repute.

The Ras Tafarian who came to my plantation to work seemed to me, after I had interviewed him, to be a genuine one. The workers on my farm at first took the view that he should only be allowed to work if he cut his hair. But I managed to persuade them out of this unreasonable attitude. The only name I ever knew the Ras Tafarian by was the generic "Brother Man," for he would give us no other.

From the very start, after I had gotten over the shock of Brother Man's appalling appearance, I took a special liking to him. To begin with, he had an excellent, rather impish, sense of humor. Secondly, he was a good musician. He had a large Milanese-type mandolin which he had made himself. It was beautifully hand-carved and decorated on its rounded back. He had strung it like a guitar. With this strange instrumental crossbreed he would accompany himself as he sang in a soft, fine tenor.

He carried his mandolin wherever he went—even into the fields when he was working. He worked well, but he soon found that he could ease his labors on occasion by offering to sit in the back of my jeep as I made my rounds, playing and singing for me. I was only too glad to make myself an easy mark.

I soon discovered that Brother Man was an habitual do-gooder, but he was not a do-gooder in the aggressive way of most such. He had a genuine love and concern for people, and he was always unobtrusively doing good turns for workers on the farm. One day he did a good turn for me with odd consequences.

One evening Barbara and I gave a large party at Charlottenburgh for assorted visitors and expatriates. About forty people were invited, including the Earl and Countess of Mansfield, Noël Coward and his party, and my old friend Ian Fleming. Things were going along pleasantly when, at about eight o'clock, while I was in the pantry helping with the drinks, I heard some noises of alarm coming from the front verandah. As I went to see what the trouble was, a thin, nervous English lady on her first visit to Jamaica came rushing up.

"Come quickly!" she said breathlessly. "Three desperate-looking cutthroats have invaded us!"

When I got to the verandah a strange sight met me. On one side of the veranda about twenty of my guests were backed up against the wall looking most alarmed. Facing them from the other end were indeed three of the most villanous-looking "Dreads" it was possible to imagine. One of them was Brother Man.

"Good evening, Brother Man," I said.

"Evening, Boss. I hear you have a party tonight so I bring my friends to play you a little music."

And play music they did, under the almond tree on the lawn. As soon as my guests understood that the desperate "natives" were not about to cut their throats, they relaxed. Noël sang, accompanied by Brother Man. We got folk songs and we got reggae. Everyone danced. Brother Man passed reefers around, to Nöel's great disapproval, for he was strongly against pot. Everyone became a bit too relaxed. And the best party I ever put on ended at two in the morning. Mungo Mansfield—the Premier Earl of Scotland—and Brother Man—the Premier Ras Tafarian of Charlottenburgh—had become the best of friends.

One day Brother Man came to me and told me that he felt someone should be looking after Miss Mumma and her family.

"She need man, Boss. I moving in with her. She will rest in peace if I bring to her the love of Jah."

So Brother Man moved in with Miss Mumma and, certainly, she was all the happier for it. He had done yet another good deed.

4

Vexing problems developed.

When Miss Mumma had first arrived, her two small boys were about eight and ten years old. They were both retarded. The younger one never learned to speak properly. He'd jabber away in a kind of baby talk which I found quite unintelligible though his mother and Brother Man seemed to be able to understand him. He would fly into rages from time to time, and as he grew older he would threaten people with stones or cutlass, though he never actually carried out any of the threats.

The older brother spoke more clearly, though with a very limited vocabulary. He grew up into a big, strong fellow who gave the appearance of glaring sullenly at the world. But he had by far the milder nature of the two. By the time these two boys reached their late teens, they started, like their mother, to have periods when they went around the bend entirely, and I had to arrange for them to be arrested, too, so that they could get treatment.

The daughter, who was the youngest of Miss Mumma's three children, was the only one of the family who never actually went off her head. She was not seriously retarded, but was simple-minded and irresponsible. She was a well-built girl, quite attractive in appearance, with the inevitable consequence that she gave birth to her first child at fourteen. I tried to find out who the father was, but never succeeded.

My farm manager said, "We will never find out because everyone knows she fool-fool. And all the boys at Aleppo 'vantage her. When she sit on so many prickles, she can't know which one prick her." And the prickles kept on pricking her; she had another child before she was sixteen; and another at seventeen. Brother Man was very upset about it, but could no nothing with her. Then we discovered that her first baby was virtually an idiot.

Quite clearly, the whole business of Miss Mumma and her family was getting out of hand. I was convinced that the daughter, if left to her own devices, would soon populate the island with idiots or psychotics.

After having Miss Mumma arrested for the fifth time, and the two sons for the second time in order to get them treated, I managed to find out the name and the dosage of the drugs with which they were treated in the hospital. With the help of a family doctor who gave me a prescription for them, I put in a large, private supply. This led to the second offense in my developing life of crime, which was administering drugs without medical qualifications. But the process of having to get poor Miss Mumma and her two sons arrested and locked up, sometimes for as long as three or four days before the

DMO could get around to certifying them, seemed barbarous. The conditions in Jamaican lockups are disgusting. They would be caged in tiny concrete cells; their food, such as it was, pushed in to them in the sort of cheap metal pan which I used to feed my dog. There they stayed, filthy and neglected, often screaming the place down until the DMO arrived and they were sent off in the Black Maria.

From the day I got my illegal supply of drugs, I never had to send them to the mental hospital again. When they started to show signs of relapse, I would dose them; and this, more often than not, aborted any major attack. I did not, however, earn my skill as an amateur and illegal doctor without some trial and error. On one occasion when I got to Miss Mumma too late and she was fully into her hymn-singing manic phase, the usual dose just bounced off her. So I gave her a slightly larger dose, but this didn't work either. The following morning I gave her a double dose. And then when I went to her cottage later in the day, she had disappeared.

I had the ranger and Brother Man make a search for her. They couldn't find her. Nobody could tell me where she could be found. I put three more men onto the job, and they searched until dark. Still no Miss Mumma. I began to have visions of the terrible consequences which I would suffer at the hands of the law if something had happened to her and I was prosecuted for dosing her illegally. I could, after all, have killed her. Not being a doctor I would not be solidly defended by medical colleagues all giving expert evidence that her death had been caused by some quite unrelated factor.

I was greatly relieved when, the next day at five in the afternoon, she was found safe and well, curled up on a pile of banana trash in one of the more remote banana walks, fast asleep. She had been sleeping for about twenty-four hours. When she awoke she was her cheerful, normal self and thanked me for having been such a remarkable and successful doctor. The margin between fame and disgrace is slim.

But all this wasn't solving the problems of Miss Mumma's simple-minded and chronically pregnant daughter. She was now pregnant for the fourth time, and it was obvious that the boys from Aleppo would continue to take advantage of her for some years to come. The farm manager reported that the second child was now old enough to be tested, and that he was as half-witted as the first. So I visited the doctor friend who had given me the prescription and told him about this new problem.

It was clear, he said, that in any civilized society she would be allowed an abortion, and she'd also have her tubes tied off. But abortion by choice is illegal in Jamaica, and before a doctor will tie off a woman's tubes he rightly insists upon her consent in writing. Miss Mumma's daughter could not read or write. Neither could Miss Mumma. It would also be quite impossible to explain to Miss Mumma's daughter what having her tubes tied off entailed. At the kind of level at which I had to operate, matters of rational explanations and written consents were irrelevant.

In due course I arranged an illegal, expensive, but safe abortion. And this having been uneventfully accomplished, my doctor friend, who happened to be a surgeon, tied her off. I had added the illegal procurement of an abortion to my ever-growing criminal record. And, as I had signed the consent at the time of the surgery, probably forgery as well.

What worries me as I write this is what is to happen to Miss Mumma and her family if I am not here to dose them with the drugs they need? One trouble is that I have exhausted the supply of the proper drugs; and my doctor friend, like so many thousands of people of all classes, has now left Jamaica in disgust.

This is not the first time I have run out of supplies, though I have found as another example of trial and error that thirty milligrams of Valium daily will control Miss Mumma and her sons if I get them early enough. Valium seems to be the fashionable tranquilizer at the moment. I took one five-milligram tablet once, and it made me feel confused. I cannot bear to think what thirty milligrams would do to me. I do not propose to try. Yet, the doctors are shoveling it into their patients by the ton. In a few years they will probably discover it makes one's grandchildren grow two heads.

I wonder if they have tried it out on laboratory mice? I have a theory that everything gives laboratory mice cancer. I think they get cancer as their only means of escape.

"The Surgeon General," I read on packets of American cigarettes, "has determined that cigarette smoking is dangerous to your health." Good for the Surgeon General. But so are a lot of other things. What about motor cars? Or bottles of whiskey? Or crossing the road?

There was a report in the newspapers not long ago of a young woman who drank herself to death on water. So water can be dangerous. And what about joining the Armed Forces? Or that act, which once committed, invariably ends in death? I refer to being born. It seems to me that when it comes to cigarettes the Surgeon General *is* determined, rather than *has* determined, that it is dangerous to health.

I light a cigarette in defiance of the warning on the pack, for it is an American cigarette from a small hoard that a friend brought me as a gift from New York. I have no doubt that cigarette smoking increases one's chances of getting cancer or emphysema or heart attacks. But how do we measure the good effects of smoking? Nobody as far as I know has tried to do so. So how do we know that the good effects do not outweigh the bad?

The Surgeon General of the U.S. is entitled to his opinion, and I to mine. I am grateful for his well-intentioned warning, but it makes me apprehensive. There is but a short step nowadays between the official belief in the harmfulness of a drug, and its prohibition.

Our ancestors lived in a theological world in which the

authorities prescribed what beliefs were harmful to our immortal souls. According to their own lights, the Inquisitors were not wicked or cruel to torture heretics to get them to recant. How much better it was to subject a person to a few days or even weeks of torture if at the end of it he gained eternity in the Kingdom of Heaven. But then at last the principle of religious freedom was accepted and eventually became enshrined in the American Constitution, a religious freedom which allowed people to go to Hell or to Heaven in their own way. Along with this went freedom of speech and writing so that the State no longer controlled what men were allowed to put into their heads.

But no sooner was the spiritual authority of the State cut down to size than a new authority was established: that of scientists. No sooner had we gained the right to put what we liked into our minds, we lost the right to put what we liked into our stomachs. The religious authoritarianism of a former age is now clear to us in all its cruelty and absurdity. Our medical authoritarianism is equally absurd, but it is difficult for most people to stand aside and view with detachment that bit of history in which they are presently immersed. We enjoy a pitying laugh at the idea of a former age hotly debating how many angels can dance upon the point of a pin. Not many of us can see the absurdity of trying to "cure" a heroin addict by addicting him to methadone instead; or banning certain drugs for general sale because they could be used to commit suicide, while freely allowing the sale of guns or even the free ascent to the tops of high buildings from which would-be suicides could quite easily jump off.

Marijuana, called "ganja" in Jamaica, was introduced by the Indians over a century and a half ago and immediately became the butt of hostility and outrage on the part of the Colonial rulers and that small section of the population which shared their beliefs and prejudices. It was made illegal, and to its use was attributed every kind of crime and vice. In spite of this, the use of ganja as a social drug became and remained widespread among the Ras Tafarians and the working classes.

The advantages of ganja as a medicinal herb were also understood, and such was the strange dichotomy of Jamaican society that my old Nanny Elizabeth Selvyn always kept an infusion of ganja in a small bottle and dosed me with it whenever I had a cold on my chest without my parents suspecting that she possessed such a thing or that, indeed, it could be used for the relief of bronchial congestion.

5

I live in a society in which, for a century, half the men in Jamaica have used ganja as a social drug without there ever having been a single case of escalation to hard drugs. Yet, there are still vicious laws against its use or sale. The upper-class prejudices against ganja were reinforced when the Ras Tafarians began to use it for religious purposes. In the late fifties I began to assail this prejudice in my column in the *Gleaner* * and in broadcasts. And after a good deal of initial outrage from the police and the "respectable" members of

* *The Daily Gleaner* is the largest and oldest daily newspaper in Jamaica.

society, a number of other writers joined me, and it looked for a while as if we were making some headway towards the legalization of ganja.

Unfortunately for us it was about this time that the demand for marijuana in the U.S.A began to increase greatly, and a vast illegal trade developed between Jamaica and Miami. Private aircraft would come in by the dozen from the U.S.A., pick up tons of compressed marijuana, and fly back to Miami with it.

The American authorities, finding it difficult to control these smuggling operations in the U.S.A., prevailed upon the Jamaican government to pass even more stringent laws, and, with the aid of American agents, Coast Guard ships, and assorted electronic equipment, to declare open warfare against the ganja smugglers in Jamaica. American and Jamaican prejudice thus combined to reduce to a trickle the large volume of a trade most lucrative to Jamaica.

All the reliable medical reports which I have seen indicate that marijuana is at worst no more harmful than alcohol. Yet I have learned over the years to avoid using any medical arguments in its favor, not only because they are inconclusive but because in the final analysis they are irrelevant. To begin with, in any discussion as to whether a drug is "addictive," no two people ever seem able to agree upon what the word "addictive" means.

Heroin is addictive, some say, because the withdrawal symptoms are very severe. But this is a quantitative, not a qualitative definition. People can become addicted to almost anything and suffer some degree of withdrawal discomfort. This is certainly true of cigarette smoking. And the withdrawal symptoms of the heavy drinker, with the "shakes" and delirium tremens, can be just as bad as the withdrawal symptoms of the heroin user. I have long concluded that there are no addictive drugs; there are only addictable people.

The real issue in any event is not whether marijuana or

cigarettes or whiskey or heroin or cocaine happen to be bad for you or not. The real issue is whether we are going to free ourselves of medical dictatorship.

Nobody nowadays would seriously suggest that a religion or a book should be made illegal because it contains dangerous ideas which might be bad for us. We have assumed that adults are sufficiently responsible to pick, choose, and refuse, and that in any event a person has the right to believe what he wishes, provided he does not harm others.

I fail to see why the State should interfere in the case of the drugs an adult wants to use. The doctors have no more right to interfere with our liberties than the theologians have, unless, of course, we go about frightening the horses.

I believe that all drugs, like all ideas, should be freely available to adults. I also believe that the most harmful addiction of all is demonstrated by those who are addicted to doing us good and saving us from ourselves by law. It is they who have been responsible for the creation of all victimless crimes. It was their spiritual ancestors who ran the Inquisition and who burned the witches. It is they who create and run totalitarian governments. We shall never escape from them unless we realize that as soon as they are defeated in one direction, they pop up in another.

The truth of the matter is that the problem of drugs will never be cured by law. Only free and responsible people, aware of the nature of consequences, will be able to cope with that; for much of the problem of drugs is only a problem because we have made it into a problem.

The problem of witchcraft solved itself very simply. We ceased to believe in it and in the orthodoxy which created it. It may sound odd to present ears to say that I suspect we can also solve the problem of drugs in very much the same way. Drugs can't do anything. They are only "things." It is we who have given them the evil magic.

6

I sit watching the sun go down and wonder whether I really shall have to leave Jamaica and whether, if I do, a new life in America will be any better than the kind of life to which we'll all soon be reduced. Once again I would become unknown and relatively poor. I am frightened of this; yet, I am even more frightened of the consequences of remaining, for there are only two possible outcomes of the present regime: either Jamaica will quietly sink into Haitian poverty and squalor, or there will eventually be bloody rioting. The first, I could not bear. As to the second, I do not see how I could avoid being sucked into the violence, and I despise violence.

We live in a century which specializes in displaced persons. Until now it has always been something which happens to others. Is it to happen to me? If it does, I wonder whether I shall have the courage to cope with it.

The small hawk circles around and comes in to land, flaps down, on the highest branch of the tall spathodea which rises like a red flame at the edge of the garden. The yellow acacias are in bloom too, shedding their yellow blossoms onto the golden carpet at their feet.

A scissors-tail hummingbird called the doctor bird, the national bird of Jamaica, is hovering over a flower; and two short-tailed mango hummingbirds, humming and zooming around a feeder hung on a branch of a low tree, are hotly contesting a matter of territory, their thin black beaks carried like stilettoes. I buy a pound of sugar a week for the hummingbirds. It is not nearly enough. But someone told me that I must limit the amount of sugar and water I give them. If they are allowed all they want, they won't feed from the flowers, and their diet requires the protein from the tiny insects that get mixed up with the nectar.

I certainly don't want to have a lot of malnourished hummingbirds, but there is another reason for rationing the sugar and water. They become very hostile to one another over the feeders and even more hostile to me when the feeder runs out. If I am sitting on the verandah when a feeder becomes empty, they fly at me and hover over my head like small angry helicopters, their little beady black eyes registering unmistakable indignation.

If the feeder remains empty, they soon forget their irritation and turn their attention to the flowers. If, on the other hand, I refill the feeder immediately, they drink it all up again in no time and are back with their angry importunities.

We have a small, ordinary sort of bird called a banana quit which looks like a small sparrow. I discovered that these birds also like sugar and water and tried to drink from the hummingbird feeders. At first they had no success at all unless the feeder was full to overflowing, for the simple reason that they were unable to hover. They would sit on a branch as near as they could to the feeder and try to reach it by sticking their necks out.

After a few months I began to notice a strange thing. The quits were learning to hover, if rather clumsily. Soon they were hovering quite comfortably. A few had even learned to fly backwards for a moment, a thing my bird-watching friends tell me is quite impossible for any but a hummingbird. Impossible or not, my banana quits, driven by their desire for sugar and water, had learned from the hummingbirds; and there they were, looking rather absurd as they hovered and reversed, their wings beating madly. I do not know who were most astonished, the hummingbirds or me.

Even so, the competition was a bit one-sided for the quits. However smart they were, they could do nothing to lengthen their beaks, which put them at a disadvantage when the feeders were half empty. Nevertheless, they had mastered a few unquitlike techniques, a triumph of greed and intelligence over a natural limitation.

Two days have gone by and I still haven't figured out what to do about Lurleen and her mischievous gossip about old Tom. It is really too pleasant just puttering about in the garden for any serious thinking. Besides, I have been writing all day, three columns which I should have finished yesterday; and tomorrow I must go to Kingston.

Pat, my second wife, strolls over to me in her bathing suit from the swimming pool in which my two little stepdaughters are swimming with the skill and grace of two budding Olympic stars.

"I went 'round to see Joan and Harold Phillips this morning. They and the kids are going off to live in Canada at the end of the week," Pat says. "They have a trailer there and the whole place is a mass of packing cases."

I say nothing, and Pat runs back to the pool. I should really go with her, for the two little girls like to be encouraged and Pat has a new bathing suit and is expecting admiration. But the mention of packing cases has caused memories to flood into my mind, and I want to be alone to come to terms with them. The packing cases have made me remember my old nurse and certain things about my childhood. So I go to my study, sit at my desk and take out a sheet of paper.

7

My old nurse wasn't called "nurse" of course. She was called "Nanny." Her proper name was Elizabeth Selvyn. She was short and stout and walked with the top of her body bent forward, her bottom sticking out behind because of an old hip injury. She never wore less than three petticoats and was deeply rooted in Victorian England, though she was Jamaican and black. God rest her soul. She's been dead for years.

When I was a child, leaving Jamaica for a journey abroad —even for a short holiday—involved a large number of packing cases, baskets and steamer trunks, some labeled "Cabin Baggage" in black, and some labeled "Hold" in red.

We traveled on the banana boats, owned and operated by Elders and Fyffes, which had names like *Coronado* and *Camito,* and they usually left Kingston Harbor in the afternoon. It was said that if any of them were about to sink, the lifeboats would be filled with the bananas, and the passengers abandoned.

Packing, in our household, used to start days before the date of sailing. By early morning of the great day most of the huge trunks and tin boxes had been packed, and all that remained to do was to lock them or rope them securely and load them upon the mule-drawn dray that had come for them.

Nanny, who took charge of everything so far as I was concerned, always traveled with us in those days. She had certain fixed beliefs. She believed, for example, that ship's eggs stored in waterglass were unwholesome for children. She had an equally low opinion of frozen meats, so the fourteen-day voyage to England set her a problem which she solved by having a carpenter build a large wire-mesh crate into which she put fourteen young laying hens. This crate would be moved down to the wharf by the dray, loaded onto the afterdeck and covered with a tarpaulin. The hens provided fresh eggs, and each day one would be killed for fresh chicken—the last on the final day of the voyage.

Nanny also had very strong ideas on the subject of cleanliness. With her, it was not just a question of cleanliness being next to godliness, it was right up there as the outward form of an inward grace. In any event, if anyone had asked her to define godliness, he would have defined it as something she called "good behavior."

She owned a large basket which she carried everywhere. Among the many things it contained were such items as a can of condensed milk, a bar of milk chocolate, and a pack of biscuits. It also contained a large, wooden-backed hairbrush, the bristle side of which she employed to brush my hair, whenever she could lay her hands upon me, in a constant, if more or less fruitless, effort to keep me looking "tidy."

The wooden back was used as a paddle to spank me with whenever I departed from her standards of "good behavior." This hairbrush had been accordingly in constant use in one way or another. The basket also contained a cake of soap but, in addition to this, it also contained another piece of soap which to me was much more sinister. It was a long, wedge-shape sliver of brown washing soap sharpened to a point, the purpose of which I shall explain in a moment.

But you must first know that in the twenties in England and Jamaica strong purgatives given at regular intervals were considered essential to health. It was common for people to indulge in a monthly "washout" which meant that once a month, usually on a Saturday night, they would dose themselves with purgatives of various kinds–usually cascara sagrada –and consider the whole operation a failure if it did not keep them glued to the seat of the WC for most of Sunday.

I do not know what made this heroic purging fashionable. To this day, more purgatives are sold in England per capita than in any other country on earth. I suspect the fashion may have been a consequence of the theories of a famous English surgeon, Sir W. Arbuthnot Lane, who early in this century became quite deranged on the subject of the human colon. This distinguished doctor claimed that the colon, if not the seat of Original Sin, was certainly the source of a long list of diseases by reason of a process which he called "auto-intoxication." This was supposed to be caused by the accumulation of waste matter in the colon which generated toxins which were then absorbed into the body.

Sir Arbuthnot advocated the surgical removal of the colon whenever possible. But if this radical step did not recommend itself immediately to a patient, he was instructed to keep his colon as clean as possible by regular doses of mineral oil.

This distinguished surgeon, knighted by his Sovereign and supported by his colleagues, had determined that colons were dangerous to health. I wonder what would have happened had he been an American and become Surgeon General.

The good doctor faithfully followed his own advice. He regularly dosed himself with so much mineral oil that London hostesses soon learned to take the precaution of putting special covers upon the chairs he sat on to protect the upholstery from the oil which constantly leaked out of the colonic sump of the worthy knight.

Of course, one never knows for sure which way it happened; Sir W. Arbuthnot Lane may have been an extreme product, not the cause, of the anal obsessions of the English. As I grow older, I find cause and effect increasingly interchangeable. I sometimes wonder whether the words are not semantic traps leading us into all kinds of discussions at cross-purposes.

The country in which I am as I write this, *my* country, as I have been taught to say, has recently decided in effect to have what amounts to a totalitarian government. We are, as I write, under martial law—a "temporary" measure which has been going on for five months now and will probably continue until the opposition is disorganized and intimidated. Is there a cause for this? What makes men constantly give up their freedoms, putting mountebanks and con-men in power, only to have to battle for them all over again at some future time?

Perhaps the majority of our people do not want to be free. Perhaps freedom is too much effort, too dangerous, too insecure. In which case their decision to support a government which takes away their freedom is not a cause, but an effect. Is there any useful purpose in continuing to write of values and objectives in which neither the majority nor its government is any longer interested? Much better perhaps to leave before I suffer the prosecution with which I have been thrice threatened.

I have been told by some that the values I try to uphold are purely subjective; indeed, that all values are merely determined subjectively, colored by the vagaries of class and culture, even of race—whatever race is.

It seems to have become fashionable to deny the existence of any value system or Natural Law which stands on its own over and above anyone's subjective wishes. But the trouble is that if the concept of *Natural Law* is to be logically defended, it can be defended positively only on the basis of theism, which sets a lot of problems.

One rather negative way of defending Natural Law is to take a look at the consequences of opposing it. If we take seriously the views of those who deny the existence of Natural Law, then there is no logical reason for saying life is anything but the accidental result of the random movement of particles; as if some ape, hammering away long enough at the keyboard of a typewriter, will not only write all the works of Shakespeare but will invent the universe. Nor would there be any logical reason for denying that man's mind is but a brief interlude of consciousness in a universal process of entropy. If thinking is only a biochemical effect, then our thoughts have nothing but a biochemical significance.

I have a habit of writing down odd bits and pieces of things that appeal to me, and I go to my notebook and find a paragraph I copied from C. S. Lewis. He wrote, "Every particular thought (whether it is a judgment of fact or a judgment of value) is always and by all men discounted the moment they believe that it can be explained without remainder as the result of irrational causes. Whenever you know that what the other man is saying is wholly due to his complexes or to a bit of bone pressing on his brain, you cease to attach any importance to it. But if naturalism were true, then all thoughts whatever would be wholly the result of irrational causes. Therefore, all thoughts would be equally worthless. If it is true, we can know no truth; it cuts its own throat."

It seems a waste of time to pursue truth if ultimately there is no such thing. If there is no such thing as Natural Law, then everything is pure chance or whim. So I am compelled to believe that there is a Natural Law or, if you prefer it, some kind of harmonic principle by which discords may be identified—some kind of truth which stands above and apart from us but which is there to be discovered if we have the liberty to do so.

I cannot in my column in a popular daily newspaper write it quite like that. Besides, it is not much use trying to rally an impoverished peasantry to the banner of a thing called liberty when their poverty has made a number of liberties presently unavailable to them. To at least half the people of Jamaica the deprivation of liberty means little. It is useless to tell them that even so they would be wise to support any system which leaves them *potentially* free. They have no means of measuring the corruption, the stupidity and the adminstrative incompetence of the demagogues who promise them salvation, or of understanding the ultimate self-defeat of vesting too much power in the State. If they rise in violence against their present leaders, it will be because the wealth they have been promised has failed to materialize. And this will be for the wrong reason. For given the Jamaican situation, no government can in the short term give our people wealth.

But it is time I got back to purgatives.

Medical science half a century ago could be as dangerous to the patient as the disease. Some people think it still is, though the often abused pharmaceutical manufacturers are managing to pull the fat out of the fire for the doctors. But even in this "scientific" matter of the development of new drugs, a certain dangerous arrogance can be detected. Human beings have evolved along with every other living thing on earth, sharing the same building blocks and the same evolutionary experience. No natural substance can be outside that experience, and if we describe certain natural substances as *poisonous*, we are not talking about any innate essential quality but about dosage, which is quite a different thing.

When we say that strychnine is poisonous, what we really mean is that strychnine above a certain dosage is poisonous, for in safe dosages it is a useful stimulant. Anything is poisonous given in sufficiently large dosages, even water. Not so long ago a man died from drinking too much carrot juice.

But what happens when the chemists make a wholly new substance unknown to nature? It is one thing to extract or to concentrate some factor occurring naturally in plants or animals, but a wholly new substance is entirely alien to our evolutionary experience and to bodies which are its product. There is no evolutionary memory of it; no recognition; no means of defense except sometimes to tuck it away in our bodies somewhere; in our bone marrow, for instance, where it remains threatening and unaltered.

Wholly new laboratory-made substances always will be a menace to living organisms. Only an arrogant and prejudiced pharmaceutical industry could have produced thalidomide while neglecting the safer, natural advantages of marijuana. When it comes to making substances to be used exclusively as poisons, the manufactured substances are champions, as so many dangerous insecticides have demonstrated. Yet, the significance of this seems to have escaped many of those concerned with preparing drugs for human use.

These pesticides and weed killers, so effective against pests and weeds, are also exceedingly "effective" against people. As a farmer, I have every reason to know how necessary it is to control plant pests and how useful the chemical pesticides can be. As time went on, I also learned about their dangers and limitations. One of the things I did soon after buying Charlottenburg was to plant out a six-acre field in Valencia oranges, and those young plants soon punctured any arrogant belief I may have had to the effect that there was nothing much more to farming than digging a hole, planting something, and then lying back comfortably waiting for it to bear.

My first lesson came when the plants were a year old. On a Wednesday I had inspected them with pride, pleased with their vigorous growth and the mass of new young leaves they had sprouted. On the following Tuesday, I went to look at them again. There was not a leaf to be seen. The plants stood sadly, totally denuded of foliage as if assaulted by a northern winter.

The cause of this, which I should have known about earlier but hadn't, was a kind of slug particularly addicted to the young leaves of citrus plants. Thousands of them had moved in and in five nights' marauding had eaten every leaf in sight.

The local agricultural officer told me that the leaves would soon grow back provided I killed every slug immediately. This, he said, was not very difficult to do, for there was only one thing which the slugs liked to eat more than young citrus leaves. That was a mixture of metaldehyde, cornmeal and sugar. So I bought a hundred-weight of cornmeal, ten pounds of metaldehyde, and five pounds of brown sugar. I had it all mixed up with water into little balls which were scattered all over the field. That was the end of the slugs.

It was also the end of two stray dogs, six stray cats, four pigs, and all my ranger's hens.

All I can say is that the carnage was not quite as bad as when, still very inexperienced in these matters, I was persuaded by a salesman to scatter Endrine pellets over sixty acres as part of a war I was waging against rats. The result of this exercise really scared me. Those acres stank of death. Hundreds of rats certainly died, but so did every other living thing including harmless lizards and, what was even worse, a large number of birds. After that, I never set poisons in my fields again.

I still had other lessons to learn, and my first field of

oranges was still teaching me. After the leaves grew back, they were assailed by another pest, aphids, which caused the leaves to curl up as if in pain. This time, in my folly, I sprayed the leaves with a solution of dieldrin in water. This killed the aphids. It also killed all the natural predators of the aphids and all the natural predators of four other pests. So, for two years afterwards, my unfortunate orange plants suffered every pest in the book, simultaneously and one after the other. They recovered their health eventually but only after a wise frienl stopped me from pursuing each new disease with a new pesticide sold me by some enthusiastic salesman.

He said, "We've got to be prepared to share some of our plants and crops with the insects. They're entitled to a living, too, you know. Besides they don't do so much harm provided the balance is right. I never use a pesticide unless things get really hopelessly out of balance, as they do occasionally, and then only with the greatest care."

The field of oranges also taught me something about Jamaica's bitter human heritage.

When I first bought dieldrin to spray the trees, I mixed the first fifty gallons myself—a gallon of the chemical to fifty gallons of water and a small amount of emulsifier as a "sticker." I went to great trouble to explain to the three men who comprised the spray team how careful they must be in handling the stuff, taking special pains with a new man by the odd name of "Cock" who had recently asked for work on my farm. I issued them with rubber gloves and protective aprons and left them to the job under the supervision of the headman.

Later that day when the headman came to me to report, he said, "The man Cock work well, but him is a funny fellow."

"How do you mean funny?"

"Well, Boss, after you leave yesterday he pour out a mug of the spray mixture and drink it."

"Good God!" I exclaimed. "Why?"

"Cock say if Backra (white man) tell you something bad for you that means it is good nourishment. Then he drink off the whole mug before I could stop him."

I sent for Cock, to find him in the best of health. He refused to be contrite in spite of the bawling-out I gave him, and he maintained with a wide grin that the dieldrin would do him no harm at all.

He seemed to be right. His continuing good health had the affect of making the other men on the team increasingly careless in the handling of dieldrin and other chemicals and very soon they were not even bothering to wear their gloves.

Then one day Cock dropped dead. I do not know whether it was his pint of dieldrin-and-water that killed him. At the hospital where his body was taken, there must have been some kind of examination, but these things are taken very casually in Jamaica and I never could get anything out of the doctor in charge. I suspect that the dieldrin must have been tucked away in Cock's body somewhere and then for some reason suddenly reemerged to kill him. I asked the doctor about this, to be answered with a bored shrug of his shoulders.

"Any man who is damn fool enough to drink a pint of dieldrin deserves what he gets," said the doctor.

In any event, I encouraged the belief, which was generally held by my farm workers anyway, that it was the dieldrin that had caused Cock's death and there was a dramatic improvement thereafter in the care used to handle pesticides.

The early pesticides were nothing like as lethal as many now currently available. It seems to be absurd to talk about a "harmless" pesticide, for obviously the more lethal it is, the better it is from the very short-term point of view.

Yet, given the present situation in the world, it is difficult to see how the use of pesticides on a large scale can be avoided. The continuing increase in the world's population, especially in what is called the Third World, is putting ever-increasing pressure upon food supplies. This, combined with a demand by large urban populations for more "efficiency" in food production—by which is meant, of course, a drive for relatively lower food prices—is compelling farmers toward the use of more pesticides and more inorganic fertilizers whether they like it or not. The farmer who uses compost and lets the insects take a share of his crops is not able to compete.

I heartily support all those urban intellectuals who are forever hollering their heads off about the dangers of insecticides and the overuse of inorganic fertilizers; but with one reservation, which is that they recognize their own role as consumers in forcing the farmer into the methods of which they disapprove.

Nevertheless, medicine is vastly more sensible and effective today than it used to be. At one time, any ill-defined indisposition was apt to be put down as something called "a bilious attack," especially in the tropics.

When my mother became pregnant six years after she had been told by her doctor that she would never conceive, she was told that she was suffering from a bilious attack and must take exercise which would "shake up her liver." So she went to her brother's sugar estate and went on long rides on horseback, purposely bouncing up and down in the saddle. She was also, of course, bouncing me up and down on the saddle, too. It was a miracle I was not born prematurely on horseback, and I have often wondered whether my deep mistrust of horses stems from intrauterine memories.

Much more harmful, though, for bilious attacks was the enthusiastic dosing of a patient with a mercurous chloride preparation called "calomel," followed the next morning by heroic doses of Epsom salts. Those who survived such regular treatments must have had constitutions of iron.

Nanny, like everyone else, firmly believed in the importance of "internal cleanliness," but it was to her credit that some inner wisdom caused her to disagree strongly with the use of harsh purgatives. She never permitted any to be used upon me. Yet, custom prescribed that I be purged from time to time, and Elizabeth Selvyn used her long wedge of brown soap for this purpose. As this was a most disagreeable procedure, she would also threaten me on occasion with "the soap" in the event of any particularly bad behavior on my part; so that for a while, I came to equate constipation with sin.

I once mentioned this in later life to a friend who was a Freudian psychoanalyst. He looked at me askance and with genuine concern and asked me whether this early experience, which he described as a "rape," had not scorched my psyche and created an interesting assortment of sexual deviations and hang-ups. I would have liked to please him, but could think of none. While he was about it, he also asked me whether I had suffered any unpleasant consequences from having been caned on assorted occasions at boarding school. The only one I could remember was the unpleasant consequence of having to give up smoking for fear of getting yet another beating. Of course people are notoriously unable to recognize their own neuroses. We all like to think that we are as normal as apple pie, though the normalcy of apple pie, or of anything else, shares with the Kingdom of Heaven a general approval and a notable lack of definition.

My friend was a young American of the generation whose parents had been corrupted by Dr. Spock and the then fashionable misinterpretations of the views of Sigmund Freud. It was a situation which produced a vast army of noisy, spoiled brats of a nastiness unequalled at any other time in the world's history. That most of those brats eventually grew up into pleasant, sensible adults says much for the abiding resilience of human nature. They had survived Dr. Spock just as my generation had survived calomel, and as I trust the present generation will survive television. I suspect that it doesn't really matter what you do to children so long as it is done with love.

Nanny did everything with a vast love in her heart. Like

the nannies of her era, in England or in Jamaica, she was a member of an institution and a way of life which no longer exists. She was also a very great woman.

I sometimes wonder, unworthily perhaps, whether our present industrial societies combined with the more extreme teachings of women's lib will not put an end to the possibility of great women. But this is nonsense. You can't abolish great women any more than you can abolish colons. The worst you can do is to make them for a while unsuitable on good upholstery.

8

I only went to England once—before the age of 10—without Nanny in attendance, and we used to go nearly every year. This journey was when I was eight, and I got into a good deal of trouble.

This came about because of my habit of reading in the loo. Most children are gregarious, but a few like to be left alone. Ever since I can remember, I have cherished most those moments when I have been left to my own devices, and feared most those situations which threatened my privacy.

I think I might eventually have been quite happy at boarding school if I could have had a room to myself. This is seldom possible at boarding schools, partly, I should imagine, because of the cost. But I have an idea that another reason is that it is easier to maintain discipline if you herd people together, forcing a collective identity upon them and never giving them a chance to fold in upon themselves and develop as individuals. The Jamaican slave owners made the marriage of slaves illegal, violently discouraged family life, and herded the slaves into barracks for similar reasons. Jamaica has never recovered from this smashing of the family concept; and the incapacity of the descendants of the slaves to form open bonds of friendship and companionship between the sexes is one of the evil legacies of slavery which still poisons Jamaican working-class society.

Sleeping in dormitories, communal washing, studying, eating and defecating were always to me a matter of almost physical pain. I often used to ask myself: What would happen to me during a war if I were conscripted into one of the armed services? I suppose most men ask themselves how they would behave in the face of enemy fire or how they would react to having to kill. To me the idea of being surrounded day and night by my comrades-in-arms was far more frightening than being surrounded by the enemy, and I would wonder how I would survive the nightmare of institutional living. To this day, that peculiar "soiled-socks" smell of communual changing-rooms gives me a feeling of anxiety.

As a child I was given a great deal of privacy at home, and the remembered tranquility of the long hours when I was permitted to do things—or nothing at all—on my own, has been a healing factor in my life. Good memories heal. Bad memories make for illness. But, of course, one can never have too much of a good thing, and as I went along I devised various means of avoiding being disturbed when I wanted to be left alone to read.

A childhood before the coming of radio and television must seem strange and remote to most people today. Nowadays if a child wants to enjoy a story, all he has to do is to turn a knob and sit like a young bird with his mouth open and have the TV set regurgitate it into him. Neither literacy nor intellectual effort is necessary. I suppose that were I a child in these post-literate days, I would live my life glued to a TV set. As it was, I had to read my stories, and I read them whenever I could.

One of the places in which I found myself least likely to be disturbed was in the loo. This fine morning I'm thinking about, as the banana boat was passing in sight of Turk's Island on its way back to Jamaica, my mother wanted to speak to me about something. When I couldn't immediately be found, my mother, well aware of my habit of holing up in the WC, looked for me in the private bathroom attached to our suite. I was not there for the simple reason that I had discovered a much more disturbance-free place which was in the public lavatory on the lower passenger deck.

My first inkling that something was amiss with our ship was when I heard a number of blasts from our foghorn; a sudden cessation of the throb of the engines, and the clattering noise of people running up and down on deck above. Thinking that we must be sinking, I hastily finished my book and ran upstairs to see a lifeboat being lowered. Almost at the same time I found myself embraced by a tearful mother who pressed me to her saying "Thank God!" over and over again.

The long and the short of it was that my parents, unable to find me, had become convinced that I must have fallen overboard and had, in turn, convinced the captain. He had stopped the ship and was in the process of sending a lifeboat party to search the surrounding ocean. My mother's relief at finding me soon turned to anger, but what was worse was that my father, instead of getting angry, unexpectedly roared with laughter and complained to all concerned in his penetrating voice that God had visited upon him a son whose head only worked when his tail was in action. I was sent to apologize to the captain.

The captain was on the bridge, his normally roast-beef English complexion purple with anger. He roared at me that the inevitable fate of a bookworm with such perverse reading habits was that he would develop piles at an early age, which fate he would richly deserve.

This captain had a pet parrot, and it was said that it was the only creature in the world for which he had any real affection. It was a miserable, irritable parrot and had never been heard to say anything intelligible except "full speed ahead." While the captain was shouting at me, the parrot had clambered upon his shoulder and was making lunging motions at me. Suddenly, it came fluttering down in a lopsided way, one of its wings having been cut to prevent its flying away in port, and as I put my hand up the parrot fixed its beak firmly and very painfully around my right forefinger.

In trying to shake it off, I swung my arm as hard as I could and on the second try the parrot released its grip on my finger and went sailing off over the railing of the bridge, flying remarkably strongly in a kind of wing-down posture. It flew clear of the stationary ship, shouted "full speed ahead!" twice, and then slowly fluttered down onto the sea.

This appalling situation caused the captain to forget about me as he shouted to the sailors to keep on lowering the life-boat. My finger was bleeding, and I decided to hop it, but not before I heard the second officer exclaim, "The little bugger threw the captain's parrot overboard!"

The parrot was rescued, wet and more irritable than ever, but otherwise in good shape. I was not there to witness this great event. I went to my cabin and refused to move until the following day when I was once more hauled before the captain and accused of throwing the parrot overboard. What with one thing and another, I felt myself to be in disgrace as well as having been unjustly treated.

The self-serving insensitivity of extreme youth now seems to me appalling. It never occurred to me at the time that the stopping of a ship in mid-ocean involved all kinds of complexities for the captain; extra work for the crew; expenses to the owners and anxiety for everyone. Instead of understanding the captain's annoyance, I resented it; what is much worse, I continued to remember my resentment until the age of eighteen, when, returning to England from Jamaica on a banana boat under the command of the same captain, I sought to pay him back.

This juvenile revenge ten years later was built around a female undergarment no longer in general use. These garments were known as "passion killers" or bloomers. During the voyage I discovered, during an unexpected gust of wind, that one of the passengers, a very fat, middle-aged schoolmistress, wore the most baggy and voluminous bloomers one could possibly imagine. They looked more like deflated blimps. I crept into her cabin while she was at lunch and stole a pair of them. Then during the dark hours just before the dawn of our arrival in Kingston Harbor, I took this magnificent garment to a very young midshipman on duty and bribed him to attach it to the lanyard and hoist it flaglike just as we were passing Port Royal.

This was done, but the whole enterprise got a bit out of hand. This was because the lanyard got hopelessly jammed in the masthead pulley and in spite of the bellowed commands of a very angry captain, our ship sailed into Kingston Harbor triumphantly flying the bloomers from the very top of the mainmast to the total bewilderment of the port authorities who thought we must be carrying some new disease. What really hurt the captain, who was a very enthusiastic Englishman, was that for the first and last time of his life he was forced to fly the Union Jack below an alien flag.

Had he been a man of wider knowledge, he would have been doubly distressed; for the garment which took precedence on his mainmast above the flag of his country was the invention of an earnest American temperance advocate called Amelia

Jenks Bloomer, after whom the garment was named. On the other hand, it had been readily adopted by the ladies of England as an undergarment, and did as much during the flourishing days of the Empire to instill awe and astonishment into the hearts of England's far-flung subject races as the Flag, the good Queen Victoria and all the British gunboats put together. Nothing keeps subject races more off balance than the suspicion that their masters and, of course, mistresses are stark, raving mad.

That particular voyage was an odd one for me for another reason. A girl of seventeen, the youngest daughter of a well-known Jamaican family, was also on board returning home, as I was, at the end of her schooling in England. She was an enchanting creature with whom I instantly fell in love, and we had a shipboard romance which in those far-off days of innocence expressed itself by the holding of sticky hands on the sundeck after dinner. We both resolved that after our arrival in Jamaica we would see as much as we could of one another, in spite of the fact that my home was in Kingston and hers near Montego Bay.

We did meet once or twice; and then at our third meeting she told me that she would not be able to see me again.

I was very hurt by this because the change in her feelings for me had been so unexpected, and it had been the first time I had imagined myself in love. What was worse, she refused to tell me what had caused her sudden change of mind.

It was not long before I discovered the reason. She had met an older woman and had become her lover; a wonderful relationship, I might add, that lasted the lifetime of the older woman.

I shall call this older woman "Lillith" because it suits her and because it was not her real name. She was one of the wittiest and most sophisticated woman I have ever met and was also a woman of great beauty. I had reason to know her well. At the age of fifteen, coming back home on one of the banana boats for the summer holidays, I fell seriously ill with what had been diagnosed first as "galloping consumption," then as typhoid fever and finally and probably correctly as polio. I ran fevers up to 106° and became delirious. There was a doctor on the ship, but like so many such he was a very indifferent doctor taking the job for a holiday. Having made the diagnosis of "galloping consumption" and giving me, in a cable to my parents, only seven weeks to live, he didn't know what else to do except to strap my chest tightly with two leather belts in order, he said, to diminish the expansion of my lungs and so to rest them.

To add to my troubles, I had also developed a large swelling in my right armpit which had become exceedingly painful.

Lillith happened to be traveling on the ship and heard about my sorry condition. Unknown to me, she had a special interest in me, for as I only discovered years later, she had been for some long time my father's mistress. She moved into my cabin with me and nursed me through my illness, tearing off the chest belts and firmly gripping my arm and saying comforting things when the ship's doctor had to slice open the swelling without the use of any kind of anesthetic as he had forgotten to bring any on board when he had embarked at Avonmouth.

I had arrived in Kingston more dead than alive, but the real doctor who came on board to take me off in a stretcher said that had it not been for this selfless woman, I would not have lived at all.

As time went on, what must have been her natural bisexuality became focused into homosexuality, and it was at this point that my little girlfriend became her lover. It was a strange situation for a romantic and rather innocent eighteen-year-old to digest. To this day I believe that I am the only man ever to have lost a girlfriend to his father's mistress; and a mistress for whom, it should be added, the son had great affection.

My father obviously had splendid taste. So did his mistress. And so did I. Yet everyone won—except me. No, perhaps that is not true—however pleasant the enjoyment of a little self-pity may be. I gained some considerable understanding of the ways of the human heart. What more has any eighteen-year-old the right to ask for?

9

Pat went to the bank this morning to get the money for the payroll. She came back looking angry and upset.

"What's the matter?" I asked.

"Oh, it's those damn hooligans again. They've been shouting the usual obscenities at me as I drove by."

"They are put up to it, you know. Don't let it upset you," I said.

"I'll never get used to it. I just can't believe that our people can behave like that." She looked near to tears.

I said, "Come, now, it's not only the shouting. What else has upset you?"

She hesitated, then she said: "Have you heard that two JLP * suporters were murdered early this morning while they slept?"

I looked up quickly. "No, I haven't heard."

"I don't know all the details. But two men were put to guard the JLP constituency office just around the corner from here. They were found this morning. Dead. Shot through the head."

"Good God!" I exclaimed. "Are the police doing anything?"

"Nothing, as usual."

She came up to me and put her arms around me. "I am frightened for you," she said. "All those awful threatening letters and phone calls you get. They feel you are one person who might stand in their way. I sometimes think we ought to leave. You've been shot before—haven't you? Before we met . . ."

That had been quite an experience.

I had a house in the hills above Kingston, in an area called Stony Hill. It was fifteen hundred feet above sea level, overlooking Kingston and Kingston Harbor. My first wife and I had used it when we had to be in Kingston. One evening at about 8:30 the maid said she thought she had seen a man prowling about the grounds so I had gone out with my gun to take a look. I saw nobody and had gone back into the house. I was on my way to my bedroom to put up the gun when I heard a scream. I rushed back into the dining room just in time to se the maid and Barbara burst through the swing door which divided the dining room from the pantry. As they came through, there was a sound of an explosion and a puff of dust as a bullet buried itself in the opposite wall.

I shouted to Barbara and the maid to lie flat on the ground, and I waited with my gun for the appearance through the screen door of whoever was doing the shooting.

* Jamaica Labour Party

No one came.

It was dark outside, and all the lights in the house were on. The jalousie windows were open. We were like goldfish in an illuminated tank for anyone prowling outside. I knew instantly that what I had to do was to get the windows closed and the lights off.

There was no door between the dining room and the sitting room. The front door opened into the sitting room and was ajar. The telephone was on a small table in the sitting room right opposite the open door. I jumped to the front door and banged it shut. Barbara, with great coolness, crawled along the floor, pulled the telephone down to her and dialled the police. I then got the windows in the dining room and sitting room closed, and turned off the lights in both rooms.

A passage led from the sitting room to the rest of the house, and there were two open jalousie windows along it. I went to the first to close it. As I did so, there was another crack of a revolver being fired.

From watching films and TV we have all become used to a sort of mild squirting noise which guns are supposed to make. This has become a sort of artistic convention in order, I suppose, to make gunfights less alarming. The reality is quite different. A gun or a revolver makes a very loud, a very sharp, and a very alarming bang. The particular bang made by my assailant's revolver, as he fired at me from point-blank range as I stood before the window, partly deafened me. I felt as though someone had quickly pinched my left hand, in which I had been holding the butt of my gun.

As I jumped away from the window, which I managed to get closed, I wondered how it was I hadn't been hit. But not for long. Barbara, who had finished the call to the police, said, "My God! Your hand is bleeding!"

So it was. As far as I could see, the bullet had gone right through it. I felt no pain at all.

There was no time for inspection. I charged down the

corridor, getting the second window closed, and into the bedroom at the end of the corridor. All the windows in the house were wooden-slatted jalousies except for the bedroom where the slats were made of glass. I pulled the curtain across these windows hurriedly and was turning to go back into the corridor when I heard another bang, a crash of glass and, simultaneously, felt as if someone had kicked me in the backside.

I banged the bedroom door and locked it from outside. I now had a narrow corridor with the windows closed, the only entrance to which was at the far end leading into the sitting room, so I got Barbara and the maid to crawl on their stomachs down the corridor, and backed them up against the locked door of the bedroom. I then crouched in front of them with my gun. There was only one way the gunman could now reach us. That was to enter the corridor from the far end, in which case I was bound to get him first.

And so we waited for the police to arrive. After ten minutes had gone by and we had heard no sound, I did a silly thing; I opened the jalousie next to me to take a look. As I did so a head popped up in front of me. The fellow must have been waiting outside the window for me to do just that. Even so, I could have gotten him if I had been quick enough. I swung my gun 'round to the window and let fly, but I was too late. My left hand, I then discovered, was partly paralyzed, which had slowed me down.

Then the police arrived. Two cars of them. And armed men poured out of them.

When they got to us, I had time to look at the damage to my hand. There was no bullet in it. The bullet had driven a neat, clean hole through it. It was bleeding—so was my bottom. When we inspected that, there was a ragged hole in my right buttock about the size of a fifty-cent piece. The bullet had flattened itself on the glass window on its way through. In consequence it had not penetrated deeply, only about an inch. In my rushing about, the bullet had dropped out. We found it on the floor. Where the other bullet had gone remained a mystery.

About fifteen minutes after the police arrived and we were trying to get things sorted out, we heard the report of a gun from just below us on the same road. The inspector in charge, accompanied by three of his men, rushed off in one of the cars.

He was away no more than about twenty minutes. When he came back he looked shaken. I poured him a stiff drink, having just downed one myself, and I noticed his hand was trembling as he reached for the glass.

"That bastard has just killed a man," he said, "in the house just below. The murdered man was sitting watching TV and the gunman shot him dead from behind. The body was lying on its face when I arrived. I turned it over with my foot. I found it was an old friend by the name of DaCosta whom I had not seen for years. I did not even know he was living there. We used to room together in Trinidad when we were students. I was very fond of him."

"I'm very sorry," I said.

"We'll catch the bastard, though. The whole area is ringed with police. We have two hundred men out. The commissioner himself is in charge."

At that point a friend arrived and drove me into Kingston to a hospital called Medical Associates. As we entered, four doctors and a group of nurses rushed forward. The head of the hospital, an old friend, cried: "Good God! Am I glad to see you! It has just come over the TV news that you were shot in the head and killed."

My wounds were relatively trivial. The specialist who examined my hand said that had he wished surgically to bore a similar hole it would have taken him half an hour of careful work to avoid all the important nerves and blood vessels—which the bullet had most considerately done.

They dressed my hand and buttock and sent me home.

When I reached home, however, there was pandemonium. My daughter Veronica had heard the news in her flat in Kingston and had driven up to our house in hysterics. She had arrived a minute or two before I returned from the hospital. I forgot all my own troubles in the effort to calm her down. Then friends from all over began to pour in. The inspector returned to say that the gunman had been caught. So we had quite a party.

The next morning my old friend John Hearne, the writer, came in. We were discussing the mystery of the disappearance of the bullet which had gone through my hand. Then he said, "By the way, what sort of gun do you have?"

"It's a single-barrel repeater shotgun," I said.

"I haven't seen one like that for ages."

"I'll go and get it for you," I told him.

It was then that we discovered the solution to the mystery of the missing bullet. In the confusion of the evening before, I had put away the shotgun without anyone noticing that the bullet had buried itself in the shotgun butt, splitting it. Had it not been for that—for I had been holding the gun in my left hand across my chest—the bullet would have entered my heart. At that point, for the first time, I got an attack of the shakes.

The gunman, it subsequently turned out, had committed fourteen burglaries, eight rapes and three murders for certain. He was twenty-five years old. He never stood trial.

One morning at 7:30 the commissioner of police phoned me. "Thought you might like to know," he said, "that your man is dead. He was shot and killed an hour ago attempting to escape."

A not unpredictable outcome, I thought.

So now I said to Pat, "Oh, that was a long while ago, and the man was a criminal, not a political gunman."

"They use criminals, you know," she said. "Do you think we shall have to leave Jamaica?"

"I hope not," I told her. "And if we do, it won't be because of threats. It will be because I can do nothing more. We shall just have to wait and see."

"Oh well, we'll just hope for the best." And Pat walked away, her face a sea of emotion.

Jamaica had been my whole life—and hers.

It seems, now that I come to think of it, that too much of my life has been spent leaving Jamaica. But paradise is like virginity: it can only be lost once. And I rather think that my personal paradise was lost many years ago.

10

There are certain things which are not fashionable to mention nowadays in spite of the fact that we pride ourselves that there is nothing we cannot say. We feel that we have put religion and sex in their proper places; chiefly, I suspect, by diminishing the one and exaggerating the other. We place great score upon our scientific approach, but in the process of debunking our orthodoxies we create new taboos.

It is not, for example, intellectually respectable to admit to a happy childhood. One is supposed, nowadays, to emerge from childhood a bleeding mass of psychological scar tissue caused by parental villains who stand condemned whichever way they plead—either for selfish overprotection or insensitive neglect. Since we are no longer allowed to blame our sins upon the Devil, we blame them upon our parents or upon our environment because, of course, it would be quite intolerable to blame them upon ourselves. That remarkable insight into human nature—the doctrine of Original Sin—is now discarded by many.

Nevertheless, unfashionable as it is, truthfulness compels me to say that I had a very happy childhood indeed. The word *love* can be the most misleading of all words. I don't suppose that a child loves his parents in a fully adult sense. He *needs* them. But as far as any child is capable of love, I loved my parents equally, though for different reasons and without qualification. It was marvelous just knowing that they were around, and it never occurred to me that there would come a time when they would not be.

But, of course, that time had to come. It came when, at the age of ten, I was sent to a boarding school in Jamaica which was supposed to be run along the lines of an English public school. The trouble was that the English public school system it copied was that of a century earlier, as it was imagined by a Colonial overseer who had never been to one. It was a windy, brutal place set on the top of a mountain miles away from any form of civilization.

The headmaster was a drunken bully who believed in flogging as an essential aid to teaching. He was greatly admired as a teacher, and his pupils, terrorized into enormous feats of brute memory, did, in fact, achieve an enviable record in the passing of examinations. He taught me Scripture, among other things. We had to stand on our benches and, in turn, recite parrot-fashion the Gospel chosen for that year's examination, while the headmaster, cane in hand, stalked threateningly between the ranks of his terrified Christian soldiers. All set books, including the plays of Shakespeare, were crammed into us in that manner. In consequence, it was a long time before I began to understand, much less to appreciate, any of them.

The desolation which swept over me on my arrival at Munro College is something that I shall never forget. I had never left home before; I felt my parents had deserted me. A lump of lead formed in the pit of my stomach and remained there, solidly and permanently. I must have held the all-time school championship for marathon weeping during my first term. I was ashamed to be seen weeping in public so I would go whenever I could into my old place of refuge, the lavatories, to enjoy a quiet cry.

I cannot use the term "WC" for the sanitary conveniences at Munro College. Water played no part in them. For the main section of the school there was a long row of some fifteen or twenty wooden seats with holes cut in them, housed in a long whitewashed wooden shed with a roof of corrugated iron.

Beneath the holes there were buckets. An elderly black man, known as "Shithouse Sam," had the job of removing and emptying the buckets. Shithouse Sam's almost obsessive dedication to his work created a hazard: for when he decided that the buckets should be removed for emptying he did not in the least concern himself with whether the seat above was occupied. There would be a sudden scraping noise, and the occupant, looking down between his legs, would find that his bucket had disappeared. There was nothing for it but to hold fire until the bucket was replaced.

There were other hazards. The whole place stank. It was infested with flies which would land by the dozen upon bare ass, penis, and scrotum as soon as one's trousers were dropped. This was no place for reading or weeping.

Fortunately I had been housed, not in one of the dormitories in the main building, but in a small house about four hundred yards away called "Morton York House," in which there were four small dormitories for about eighteen boys. The house was called Morton York House for the good, if obvious, reason that the second master, The Reverend Morton York, lived there. He was a tall, thin Englishman. His wife was a large, dominating woman with a jaw like the prow of an early twentieth-century man-o'-war who enjoyed the singularly inappropriate name of Mimi. I must assume that being the wife of an Anglican parson she read the Bible, but the only reading matter I ever saw in the house was the weekly overseas edition of London's *Daily Mirror* and a trashy women's magazine called *Home Chat.* These together with a boy's magazine called *The Champion* were virtually my sole reading at school for three years if one excludes the set books learned by heart.

The great thing about Morton York House was that it possessed a small outhouse—a one-seater—which, though based upon the bucket principle, did not smell and was not fly-infested chiefly because it was meant for emergencies only and was hardly ever used. The best part of it was that it had a door so it was the only place at Munro College in which privacy was possible. Whenever I could, I disappeared into the one-seater and wept. I must have wept at least once a day there for three months in chukkars of fifteen minutes or so, for it was not safe to remain there longer.

11

After my first term I managed to overcome the chronic weeping, but I never succeeded in shifting the lump of lead. I should, I suppose, have told my parents how miserable I was; they never suspected it. I knew that my father was very keen on my going to Munro, and I did not want to disappoint him. I wrote weekly letters home saying what fun it all was.

I soon got into the habit of leading a sort of double life. I would go through the motions of being a cheerful Munro boy, but it was all play-acting and unreal. The real me, constantly aware of the lump of lead, looked on in misery and boredom. And sometimes in disgust.

There were at Munro traditional initiation ceremonies for new boys. One was known as "candle-greasing." While the poor little wretch was asleep, the older boys in his dormitory would light a candle and drip melted candle grease all over his head. It took days of combing and cutting to get the stuff out.

Another was "crowning." The new boy was made to sit on the end of his bed while a chamber pot filled with urine was rammed down over his head like a hat. He then had to get up and declare, "Rex poniarum sum!" I am the King of the pony pot! This was considered good clean fun by all.

Then, of course, there was the headmaster, Wagger Harrison. He was a fat, coarse man who shouted at everyone at the top of his voice. A slight mistake in answering a question in class invited a thrashing. But his real talent for inflicting grievous bodily harm came to full flowering in his public floggings. About once a term, sometimes more often, the whole school—a hundred and twenty boys and a dozen staff—would be brought together in the assembly hall to witness a public flogging. This would be for some offense considered particularly serious, such as having been caught smoking, or for having pinched a few test tubes from the laboratory, or for having been found out of bounds without permission.

The whole procedure followed an established routine. Wagger Harrison would appear upon the stage and call for silence. He would then make a short speech describing the offense for which his victim was to be punished and point out how necessary it was to make an example of him. The sinner would then be marched on, surrounded by four boys chosen from the fifth or sixth forms. These would then grab the wrists and ankles of the offender on a signal from the headmaster and spread-eagle him face down over a large table set center stage.

He would be held in this position while Wagger flogged him, raining down blows from his cane along the back of his legs, his backside, and sometimes on his upper back. But the kidney area would be carefully avoided. Twelve blows would usually leave Wagger puffing and panting, and the victim would be released to go to the school matron to have his wounds dressed. He would carry the welts for a month.

I did not know it at the time, but in retrospect I realize that I was watching in Wagger Harrison the technique of the true despot. During his lifetime and after his death, to this very day, Wagger is regarded as one of Jamaica's great headmasters. Very many of his old boys venerate his memory. Their reaction to any criticism of Wagger is almost violent.

Many years after I left Munro, I received a letter from an old friend who had been at Munro College with me, inviting me to an old boys' dinner in special memory of Wagger Harrison. I politely refused, but made the mistake of explaining that I would feel myself a hypocrite to attend a dinner in honor of the memory of a man I considered to have been a vulgarian and a bully. I was quite taken aback by the vehemence of my friend's reaction. It was about a year before he could bring himself to speak to me again.

Wagger's technique was founded upon instilling intense fear in every boy who passed through his hands. It is this intense fear upon which the loving of Big Brother is inevitably based. Of course, fear alone is not enough. It has to be alternated with gentleness so that in the sudden relief of tension love and gratitude rush in. It is an intensely irrational process, for why anyone should be grateful to another for relieving a tension and a fear he created in the first place is beyond rational explanation. I suppose it is an extension of the process of relief and pleasure which one is supposed to experience when one ceases hitting himself on the head with a hammer. Irrational or not, the process of alternating brutality with kindness is a technique well known to inquisitors and torturers of all kinds.

Wagger was also an excellent school politician. He selected for special attention certain families whose wealth or influence he needed. He would proceed as usual with the process of terrifying their sons, but had these sons but known it, they were permanently exempt from flogging. Then having terrified these chosen sons, he would proceed to pamper and charm them.

At the age of eleven, I experienced a personal example of this. A friend and I had been running about behind the chapel one day making a tremendous noise. This had been disturbing Wagger in his study nearby. The next thing we knew, Wagger was confronting us, bellowing like bull. He marched us into his study and, once there, he made us stand at attention before his desk. Without a word, he then went to a rack on the wall from which hung his large collection of canes. He carefully selected the largest, holding it at either end in both hands as he tested it for flexibility.

By this time, certain that we were going to be thrashed, we were both trembling with fright. Still flexing the cane, Wagger came toward us and shouted, "You know what I'm going to do with you–don't you!" As we remained silent he shouted again, "You know what I'm going to do with you, don't you? Go on. Answer me!"

"You are going to beat us, sir," my friend managed to say. Upon which Wagger's fierce, coarse face suddenly transformed itself with laughter.

"You are wrong," he said. "You are going to have some tea and biscuits with me." And he put the cane down, put his arms around us, and took us onto his verandah. We did not know that because our fathers were well-known lawyers, we were not on his beating list.

After that incident, Wagger Harrison became almost a god to my friend. I suppose the whole process would have had the same affect upon me but for my now chronically split personality. The real me, the one with the permanent lump of lead, surveyed the whole scene with steady loathing, and this included Wagger Harrison in any mood—good or bad—and any kind of Munro tea party.

Even Wagger Harrison's public thrashings were conducted in a politcal manner. His short speeches before one of these public thrashings were brilliant mixtures of audience flattery and intimidation. By the time he was finished, he had practically everyone in the school on his side, screaming for blood. The friends of the boy to be beaten would betray their friendship by agreeing that he deserved it. Wagger made public beatings the most popular entertainment at Munro College. All the herd instincts—the cruelty, the need for hero-worship, the admiration for physical strength—which boys and savages have in common, were turned by Wagger into a cult. Even the unlucky victims of his cane would more often than not go back to worshipping him when their wounds healed, in return for a crumb or two of kindliness carelessly thrown in their direction.

The young are great conformists. It was not fashionable at Munro to dislike Wagger and, in any event, dislike would have felt like a challenge. One does not challenge God. God must be loved; especially a god of wrath.

Somehow I managed to serve out my allotted three years at Munro. With only one person there in those three years did my divided self ever come together for a while. That was The Reverend Morton York. He was the only man who taught me anything other than something remembered parrot-fashion, for he was the only person from whom I would accept anything. To Wagger the great teacher I was most of the time determinedly deaf. But The Reverend Morton York's coaching enabled me to pass, at twelve and a half, the competitive examination which took me to Stowe School in Buckingham, England. Not that I have much reason to be grateful for that. My gratitude to Reggie, as the good parson was called, really comes down to the fact that in my childish view at the time and in my more mature view since, he was the only civilized man in the whole place.

I went to Stowe just before the age of fourteen, in the winter term. In those days nobody had yet heard about cultural shock. But if you want to know what cultural shock feels like at firsthand, try being a thirteen-year-old West Indian with a tendency towards acute homesickness, arriving during the winter term at an English public school. That winter was the first time I had had to say goodbye to Jamaica for anything more than a holiday abroad with my parents.

Now, nearly half a century later, I might have to say goodbye again. At any rate, on this occasion there is no lead in the pit of my stomach, and I am all in one piece. I have been all in one piece now for a long time, but for some years after Munro and Stowe I was not. Getting it all together had been the essential struggle of those years.

I have two brothers alive, both called John. This comes about because one of them is my half-brother. I also had another brother who died, called Peter. In many ways I have been envious of all three. I am closest to my half-brother possibly because, not being wholly a brother, he is more different from me than the others. Nothing is more difficult than to forgive others for having one's own defects, unless it is to admire them for having what one fancies to be one's own virtues.

I had been envious of them because, in their different ways, they had the sense which I did not have to protect themselves from boarding schools. The most successful in doing this was John the half-brother. Nobody in Jamaica was ever such a master of the art of running away from school. He ran away from all the best schools in Jamaica. His longest session at any school was at Munro College. When he had been there for five months, three weeks, and two days, he took off one night determined to walk or to bum rides back home, one hundred miles away. After an hour's walking he saw the lights of a car and stopped it to ask for a lift. It was his misfortune that the driver of the car happened to be one of the assistant masters, so he was captured and taken back to school where, the following day, he became the victim of one of Wagger Harrison's public floggings. This was some ten years after I had left because there is a wide gap of years between us, and I gather it was one of Wagger's last super-shows. That was enough for John. After taking four days to heal, he took off again, this time for good, and nobody ever got him back to school again. As John is among the more civilized and better educated people I know, and a self-made millionaire into the bargain, I am tempted to conclude that the advantages of a formal education are overrated—at least for the highly intelligent.

My brother Peter, the one who died, was also successful in avoiding the peculiar tortures of an English public school. Hardly had he arrived at Dover College in England, than he ran away. The police eventually found him after two weeks, holed up somewhere near the West India docks in London trying to stow away upon a ship bound for Jamaica. Shipped back home, he was privately tutored until the Second World War, when he enlisted in the RAF.

My youngest brother, the other John, managed to avoid all but a short time at Munro College. Instead, he went on to an American university, became a Doctor of Medicine, and now pursues a lucrative practice in California.

Why was it, I asked myself, that I broke myself into pieces and very nearly crippled myself for life enduring something which was not worth enduring? I don't know. I do know that I suffered a broken heart long before the age at which broken hearts are supposed to be suffered. The term "a broken heart" is, of course, absurd and rightly confined to the more old-fashioned, sentimental novels. But I do not know what other words to use to describe that kind of despair beyond the reach of the therapy of tears, caused by some loss for which there can never be compensation.

As we grow older, we learn to hedge our emotional bets; to gain a multiplicity of interests; not to put all our feelings into one basket. But I did not know any of this at the age of ten. It was something a happy childhood had never taught me. In this respect, and in others, too, any street urchin with a drunken father and a slut for a mother had the advantage.

12

When I disembarked at Kingston all those years ago from the banana boat from whose mainmast the bloomers were flying, I was not yet an adult though I was no longer a child. In England I had passed the first of three examinations which I would have to take to become a solicitor, the profession of law having been chosen for me by my father, whose law firm had one of the most extensive practices in Jamaica.

The prospect of becoming a lawyer filled me with gloom, but as I had no sensible ideas about how I was to earn my living otherwise, there seemed no alternative but to go along with it. Six months before leaving England, I was taken away from Stowe School in Buckinghamshire and sent to one of those odd places, this one in Kent, which prepares students for the kind of examinations for which they could not normally sit at a public school. The preliminary examination set by the Law Society in England was one such.

I was glad to leave Stowe and to feel that my wretched schooldays were nearly at an end. This is no criticism of Stowe, which I believe to be one of the best and most enlightened of English public schools. At the time I was there, the headmaster was the legendary J. F. Roxburgh, a tall, elegant, steely-eyed man who, in addition to his scholarly attainments, shared with the best headwaiters an infallible memory for names. I returned to Stowe for a casual visit fifteen years after I had left, and J. F. Roxburgh instantly recalled my first as well as my last name and remembered that I was from Jamaica.

There was no particular reason why he should have remembered me. My rather brief stay at Stowe was not in the least distinguished, except for one small achievement which on balance had merely added to my general misery. My father had for some reason considered it important to have me taught boxing, and from the age of eight I had been regularly trained by two of the best professional boxers then in Jamaica—an ex-heavyweight champion named Wint and a German middleweight who called himself Teddy Hoffmann.

I had boxed well at Munro, and by the time I got to Stowe I was pretty well versed in all the tricks of the trade, few of which would have had the approval of the Marquess of Queensberry. In those days schoolboy boxing, at least in institutions for the sons of gentlemen, was very much of the stand-upright, straight-left school. Infighting was hardly ever taught. Rough stuff in the clinches was frowned upon.

Three weeks after I arrived at Stowe the winter boxing contest was announced. My house-master suggested, in the kind of tone of voice which brooked no refusal, that I enter myself in the weight class 110 to 120 pounds. A week later I found myself in a large building which then served as cinema, theatre, gymnasium and general assembly hall, facing for my first fight a boy called Fisher.

I was by no means happy at the prospect. I felt, to start with, terribly alone amongst all the unfamiliar faces and voices and customs. Secondly, the dental profession (Harley Street version) had played hell with me. I had two front teeth which had grown crooked and I had been taken to a most expensive Harley Street dentist who was supposed to be an expert orthodontist, though I doubt whether the word "orthodontist" was in current use in England in 1928. Even if it was, the art must have been in its infancy. Indeed in England in 1928, the entire art of dentistry seemed to be in its infancy. The bad teeth of the English were notorious, and most of the dentistry available seemed to consist of extractions or the installation of badly fitting false teeth with unconvincing cherry-red imitation gums. You could always spot English people abroad in those days by their false teeth. If the teeth seemed to want to jump out at you and bite you, the wearer was English.

This so-called Harley Street specialist had put a large gold band on my upper front teeth. Attached to this band, in front of one of my offending tusks, was something that could only be described as a small gold nut through which a small bolt was screwed. The bolt projected out between my upper and lower lips and every two weeks I was sent to London to have the dentist put a quarter turn on the threaded bolt with a screwdriver.

The idea was that the pressure would eventually push the tooth back into its proper position. This contraption did not exactly enhance my appearance or my comfort. My front teeth ached most of the time. It was difficult to drink anything. I had been able to prevent the threaded bolt from chafing my top lip by fitting over it a short length of the rubber used for the valves of bicycle tires; but there was nothing I could do to prevent it from impaling my lip if I got hit in the mouth.

The boy Fisher, my opponent, was a bit older than I was and a good three inches taller, with a longer reach. The business of fighting Fisher did not appeal to me at all. To tell the truth, the prospect of fighting anyone never, at any time, appealed to me. Boxing, like going to boarding school, was one of those things which had happened to me and from which I could find no decent escape.

Before getting into the ring, I taped my knuckles as I had been taught to do, and then noticed with some embarrassment that none of the other contestants was doing this. But as nobody objected, I took my next step. After pulling on the gloves I carefully, if surreptitiously, rubbed away as much of the padding over my knuckles as I could. Then I got into the ring and took a careful look at Fisher. There was only one way to get through this fight without getting my lip painfully impaled.

The bell rang for the first round; we touched gloves, and Fisher, standing upright, came in with a straight left. I got under it and came in close, putting in a hard left to his body. This caused his head to come down low over my right shoulder. By quickly jerking my shoulder upwards I managed to give him a considerable jolt under the chin. I heard his teeth clap together.

He dropped his left arm in an effort to hit me in the clinch. As he was tall, I managed to imprison the arm under my right arm without its looking too obvious. With his left thus safely clamped, I swung him slightly and hit him, as he came around, with another left. The referee must have been blind. He shouted at us to break, and we broke clean.

One of the things that Teddy Hoffmann had drilled into me was how after a clean break to jump in again while your opponent is still going backwards out of the clinch. So I got back in a hurry while Fisher was still square to me and off guard, and this time I hit him a beauty to the stomach with my right. Poor Fisher doubled up, winded. He hit the deck forty-five seconds into the first round and stayed down until his seconds picked him up.

When I got out of the ring, one of the senior boys in boxing shorts and vest, who was a few feet away, called me over. He was hardly a boy; rather he looked like a fully grown man, beautifully muscled and with a decidedly battered-looking nose.

"Come here, Cargill," he said.

When I got nearer, he said, "You were lucky not to have been warned in that fight. You fought damned dirty!" He scowled at me in a most frightening way.

"I'm sorry," I said, not knowing what else to say.

"Do you know who I am, boy?" he asked.

I shook my head, and he said, "Well, you must be new; you're going to get to know me well. I am Clouston. I am the school's boxing captain. I fight at 185. You will join my team."

Then he smiled for the first time and said, "Don't misunderstand my views on fighting dirty, but when you use your shoulder to give someone an uppercut in front of the whole school, it's carrying things too far."

Clouston paused, then added, "You are through to the finals now, I gather. Win it as cleanly as you can. Then meet me here tomorrow afternoon. And one thing more: what are you doing with all that stuff in your mouth?"

I explained as best I could.

"Take it out right away!" he ordered. And he walked away.

I managed to obey Clouston on all points. I took off the gold band, won my final reasonably cleanly by a knockout, and met him the following afternoon.

"I watched you in the finals," he said. "You've been well taught; but you have faults you shouldn't have. You are too much on your toes. Always keep your feet flat on the ground. Also, you are not aggressive enough. Why did you wait for the third round to knock him out when you could have done it in the second? What were you saving your right for? Your old age?"

Clouston's choice of me for the school boxing team was by no means an unmixed blessing. The good part of it included the advantage of being exempt from fagging and having the privilege of training with Clouston. For R. H. Clouston became one of the outstanding amateur boxers of England, and a legend during his short lifetime. He was determined, after getting his degree, to become a professional heavyweight boxer; but World War II intervened and he became a commando instead. He was killed in action.

Clouston believed the only effective way to learn to fight was to fight people better than yourself as often as you could. He himself got into the ring with anyone that would allow him to do so: Army or Navy champions or ex-champions; punchy old pros past their best days; anyone who felt he was handy with the gloves. This belief led to a lot of grief for me and for a few others on the team. Each year a fair would come to the town of Buckingham; and in those days one of the standard attractions of fairs was a boxing ring. The master of ceremonies would show off two or three old pugilists and offer any member of the audience five pounds if he could stay upright for three rounds against the one nearest to his weight.

When such a fair came to town Clouston and two or three of us would climb out of our dormitories after bedtime and set off quietly on our bicycles for Buckingham, two miles away. The whole enterprise was against the rules, of course. Clouston would order us into the ring against one or another of the wretched old bruisers.

Clouston always lasted his three rounds, though sometimes he took a nasty beating doing so. At least half of the time, I got myself knocked cold. My nose still has a list to starboard as a result of one of these encounters, and I like to think that my incapacity properly to encompass Latin irregular verbs is not so much due to inborn stupidity, but to having had my brains slightly addled by assorted old pros with cauliflower ears.

It is a great help at an English public school to be good at some game, and boxing helped me to avoid a good deal of the unpleasantness which always besets a new boy. Stowe did its best for me. It could not be expected to assuage the loneliness, the feeling of strangeness, and the sense of loss from which I never could escape.

The six-month interlude at the institution in Kent was a pleasant one. Most important to me was that I had a room to myself at last and was freed from the public ordeal of dormitories. I made two friends, each of whom in their separate ways taught me a great deal.

One was Lawrence Durrell. He then lived near the Crystal Palace with his mother and his younger brother Gerald, and he had been sent to our institution to take the entrance exam for the Palestinian police force. I could not imagine a more unlikely candidate. He spent a good deal of his time writing poetry and was already in love with the resonances of words. He played the piano quite well by ear according to a strange system of his own involving the use of only three fingers of each hand. He was a splendid raconteur and a passable rugger player. We organized in those days what was called a "jazz band" and made a little money playing for local dances on Saturday nights.

The other friend was a lively young man from Ceylon called Cecil Jonklass. He was obviously a racial mixture of Indian and Dutch. Every move he made, from walking to playing tennis to dancing, was made with an extraordinary feline style and grace. He was at seventeen or eighteen one of the best amateur ballroom dancers I have ever seen. He was at our institution to take the law preliminary as I was, and would, in due course, return to Ceylon and to his father's legal firm.

It so happened that ballroom dancing was a hobby of mine, too. During the holidays from Stowe, I used to go when-even I could to the Josephine Bradley School of Dancing, in the ballroom of the old Knightsbridge Hotel. (It changed its name subsequently to the Normandie.) Cecil Jonklass decided that we should commercialize our hobby. Through some friend he got us a job (if you could call it that) as professional dancers at the Cafe Anglais, which many years later was destroyed by enemy bombs.

I suppose there must be many grades of the profession of gigolo. Our grade must have been pretty low down on the scale, and was certainly not romantic. We were put at a table by ourselves on those evenings when we managed to escape from the Kent Institution and come to London on a borrowed motorcycle. This was long before the era of the disco, the deafening noise, the jungle gyrations, and the terpsichorean masturbation which currently passes for dancing.

Ballroom dancing was then a male/female joint effort based upon the male chauvinist idea that the man led and the woman followed. Ballroom dancing, mainly the slow and quick fox-trots, the waltz and the tango, was somewhat formalized. There was a basic routine to be learned within the framework of which—but within narrow limits—individaul variations could be made. Otherwise individuality was mostly expressed by one's "style." The music would be provided at a place like the Café Anglais by a "name" band; many places just had a house band as they have a house pâté or a house wine. But as you went up the scale, a "name" band would be hired—a band, that is, which had a reputation in its own right, organized by a well-known bandleader.

It was quite out of the question for any reputable young woman to go somewhere like the Café Anglais by herself, but there was nothing wrong with two or three girls going together or a girl going with her mother if there happened to be no male available to take them. This is where we came in. For many girls or women who enjoyed dancing and who perhaps were up in town from the country for a few days would often go to places like the Café Anglais and dance with the resident "professionals," getting not only a few good dances but a certain amount of informal instruction into the bargain.

It didn't cost them much; to be exact, it cost them two shillings and sixpence per dance at the Café Anglais. They went to a little window, bought a ticket, and then came across to our table. We got one shilling and sixpence and the house kept a shilling. We were not allowed to sit with our customers. We had to walk them back to their tables and then return to ours; and we were not allowed to accept drinks.

Of course, things were not always so strict in practice. Often some girl or older woman would buy three tickets at once and book one or the other of us for three dances in succession. In this case we never bothered to return to our table, and we would accept something like ginger ale or a glass of beer. On the average, we made about one pound a night, for more often than not we would be tipped a shilling or two in addition to our normal fee; and a pound a night was very good pay for a seventeen-year-old in those distant days—when an excellent three-course lunch could be had for two shillings and sixpence, including half a pint of beer.

We worked hard enough for our money. It wasn't work, but a pleasure, to dance with a good dancer; but most of our customers were not good dancers. We got so that we could know at a glance which type danced upon their own feet and which upon ours. The horsey country house girls, their coming-out parties six months or so away, would come to practice their ballroom dancing. Most of them felt as heavy as the horses they often resembled, and Jonklass and I nearly suffered double hernias pushing them around. Others were rather like supertankers; an enormous amount of initial inertia had to be overcome to get them started. But you had to be careful how you got into a heel and toe spin with them, for they seemed to have no braking power at all. We had all types from eighteen to fifty, large, small, medium, some with sweaty palms, some who smelled delicious, and one or two who smelled terrible; but we took on all comers.

It was all good clean fun, alas, and though we constantly hoped to the contrary, none of our customers, some of whom became faithful regulars, ever made a pass at us. None fulfilled Cecil's fantasy of taking us to the south of France for a weekend of sin. The early thirties, in England at any rate, were days of innocence.

Larry Durrell in the meantime had a problem. How was he to contrive to fail his examination for the Palestinian police? He did not want to upset his mother by a flat refusal, but he regarded the whole prospect with terror. The trouble was that the examination was rather easy and Larry was very clever. It is more difficult to fail an exam convincingly than to pass one.

When the time came, he failed to fail, but there was still the matter of the interview. The day came when he had to go to London to face the selection committee, and we had been preparing him for this. He wore his oldest suit with a red pullover; he left off shaving for two days. We managed to get his fingernails looking grubby. It is hardly necessary to report that the Pukka Sahibs of the selection committee took one long hard look at Larry and turned him down, thus making the world safe for *Bitter Lemons* and the Alexandria Quartet.

13

So now I went back to Jamaica to face a legal career with as stiff an upper lip as I could muster. There were worse troubles to come. The paradise that I had lost when I was sent to Stowe was a child's paradise, if you happened to be a white child born to well-to-do parents, and I suppose Jamaica was something of an adult's paradise, too, if you were white and well off and developed the habit of ignoring the serpents. But ignoring serpents takes a lot of practice and is an art you must begin to learn at puberty, or whenever it is that horizons begin to widen beyond the home. I was yet to begin the lessons, and my return to Jamaica, partly grown up and seeing it for the first time with the eyes of an adult, produced a succession of shocks.

I had not realized, for example, that the Jamaica to which I was returning was an outpost of empire of the kind that could have been invented by Somerset Maugham. The country was administered by the Colonial Office in England and its representatives, the Colonial Civil Service, in Jamaica. This encouraged a certain political irresponsibility, a political unawareness, and a strange childlike quality among most Jamaican adults, whose only way of getting anything was to beg their colonial masters for it. Indeed the whole island was based upon a kind of chronic mendicancy. As there were no trade unions, an employee begged his employer for a raise of pay; and the employer for his part would have to beg the Colonial Secretary for a new road. In colonial outposts, mendicancy became a fine art and a way of life. You learned to use a set of words in your petitions, not because they had any particular meaning to you, but because you knew they had a particular appeal to your masters. You also learned how to bite the hand that fed you while conning your benefactor into the belief that it was a love-nip.

I don't suppose that in the history of the world there has ever been a class of people as honest, as dedicated, as hard-working, and as underpaid, as England's colonial civil servants and administrators. Yet the major result of their selfless administrations in Jamaica was to produce a nation of con men adept at expressing the most beautiful sentiments and giving the most convincing reasons why something should or should not be done. To this day Jamaican politicians and public men are superbly eloquent and convincing upon the subject of any of the world's or the island's problems. There is only one thing they can't do with a problem and that is to solve it. They never had to. That was the business of the Colonial Office.

The center of Jamaican social life at that time was King's House, the residence of the Colonial Governor. His Court consisted of the senior civil servants, such as the Colonial Secretary; of the legal establishment represented by the High Court judges and the Attorney General; of the heads of the Police, the Army, and the Church of England; and of such local people, Jamaican or English, who were considered socially acceptable.

You were fully in society if you were regularly invited to King's House for tennis or other such private occasions. You were partly in society if you were invited on public occasions only, and you weren't anywhere if you were never invited at all, which was the situation with 99½% of the island's people.

Jamaican high society was small, and everyone went around in carefully calculated circles dropping visiting cards upon one another. There was more in the visiting card cult than met the eye. There were large ones and small ones and if you were in mourning, cards with black edges. The size and number of the cards you left depended on certain set rules and so did whether you turned down a corner of one of them or not. I never bothered to learn the complicated etiquette of visiting cards, but I dimly remember that single men always had to call first on married couples; but on being first married or on moving to a new neighborhood, you had to wait for the older and more established married couples to call upon you and your new wife. If they did not, this was meant as a carefully calculated snub.

Within a very short time of arriving back in Jamaica, my father saw to it that I had some visiting cards printed, and I was sent forth to drop one off at King's House and write my name in the visitors' book. I also dropped cards off at all the official houses, such as the home of the Colonial Secretary, the General and the Attorney General, and at various private homes; all of which triggered off a large number of invitations to dinners and cocktail parties, at which I always met the same people and always ran out of small talk after half an hour.

Then, of course, there was the important matter of the

season ticket for the Myrtle Bank Hotel. This hotel, built and owned by the United Fruit Company, was Kingston's leading hotel; not a very exclusive rating when one considered that there were only two other hotels in Kingston. But it was a large, rambling place, well managed, with a large ballroom and a swimming pool, and was the public center of Jamaica's high society. Public is perhaps not quite the right word, for the season ticket was more or less the equivalent of membership in a club; and while the hotel was in theory open to all, the staff and the management made it painfully plain that those who did not have season tickets were not welcome.

When the manager first gave me my season ticket, which was within a week of my returning home, I was naive enough to ask him why one was necessary.

"To keep the niggers out," he bluntly replied.

I had not been home for long before I realized that in Outposts of Empire such as Jamaica, "keeping the niggers out" was a task to which the vast majority of Whites addressed themselves constantly and with considerable enthusiasm. The near-whites also addressed themselves to the task of keeping out those with darker skins, and those with darker skins in turn looked down upon those who were black.

Yet, it was even more complicated than this. For various reasons, color prejudice in Jamaica was hardly perceptible to the child. Certainly it had not been perceptible to me up to the time that I had left Jamaica for Stowe. There were many reasons for this, both general and personal.

In general Jamaica was never like the southern states of the U.S.A. Color prejudice was never legally recognized or institutionalized in any way. There were no signs upon buses or public lavatories or in any public place excluding Negroes or assigning them to certain seats. The limited voting franchise at the time was limited by possessions, not by skin color. Perhaps most important of all, the leading private schools admitted students of various colors, and at Munro College there was a large proportion of students with skins of varying darkness.

For hundreds of years the colored children of the overseers had on the whole been given a fair and sometimes a good education by their fathers, and in consequence a fairly large middle class of mixed blood had emerged. Many people in business and in the professions were colored or black. So were a number of large landowners.

In theory at least, everyone was equal in church or under the law. Such inequalities as there were in both institutions were not based on color but, as elsewhere, on the size of one's pocketbook. Color prejudice of a vicious kind certainly existed, but it was mostly all in the social sphere and not much of it would have been noticeable to a child. It was only as the child grew older that he began to see it in the form of social sanctions.

It was the period of gradually increasing awareness between thirteen and eighteen that I had spent outside Jamaica; so when I returned more or less an adult, the whole thing hit me all at once. I soon realized that while as a child nobody had complained if I had a colored boy of my own age come to my house to play, or if I went to his, it was no longer possible for me to expect to meet him at the parties to which as an adult I was now invited; nor for that matter was I expected to go out with his sister.

The social rules were quite startlingly weird. There was, for example, the case of a black man named B. M. Clark. He was a well-educated and charming man, and was among the best tennis players in Jamaica. Because of his ability at tennis and because white society put a high premium upon sports, B. M. Clark was given the right to play tennis at the most exclusive white clubs, but not to become a member. He would be invited to white homes for an afternoon of tennis. After the game he would be offered refreshments with everyone else at the tables set up at the side of the tennis courts, but he would seldom, if ever, be invited inside the house. It was possible for him to address a white male friend by his first name, but he could never use the first name of his friend's wife.

My father and my uncle were enthusiastic tennis players. Indeed they had at one time been the doubles champions of Jamaica. So we had two beautifully kept grass courts at Coniston where I was born, and tennis parties were regular affairs. I noticed soon after my return from England that B. M. Clark would quite often come to tennis, but he would go straight to the courts, play, have his courtside refreshments and then leave. He would occasionally call my father by his first name, but my mother was always "Mrs. Cargill," and to her B. M. Clark was always "Mr. Clark."

In genuine puzzlement, I asked my parents why B. M. Clark was never invited into the house like all the rest when darkness fell.

"I don't think he wants to come in," my mother said.

"But he's never been given the choice," I persisted.

"We don't mind," said my father, "but it would embarrass our guests."

"It doesn't seem to embarrass them on the court," I replied.

"Oh for goodness sake don't be so provoking," my father said impatiently. "He's a gentlemanly fellow and knows his place."

"That's what we all like about Mr. Clark," my mother added. "He'd never get bumptious and familiar like so many would. Now dear, please stop asking silly questions."

But asking silly questions, I fear, was to become a habit, and was to lead me into a good deal of unpleasantness in one way or another.

One of the main bits of unpleasantness concerned my Uncle Sidney. He was ten years older than my father, a big man, remarkably active for his years, a pillar of the church and of society, and the Custos Rotulorum of St. Andrew. He was also the senior member of the family law firm. It was to him that I was articled.

Today we all talk of law schools, especially in America. The English system was based upon the ancient idea of apprenticeship. The would-be solicitor, having passed his law preliminary, would enter into articles of apprenticeship with a senior practicing solicitor which, in theory and sometimes in practice, bound him hand and foot to his master for five years. He was entitled to no pay and could take no outside employment. He could not get married without his master's consent. His morals had to be approved by his master.

During the course of his apprenticeship, the articled clerk, as he was called, had to take three further examinations set by the Law Society of England: an intermediate examination, an examination in trust accounts and bookkeeping, and then a final examination. All of these having been passed, the master would then apply to the Supreme Court provided he was satisfied as to the behavior and character of his articled clerk, for his clerk's admission as a solicitor of the Supreme Court of Judicature of Jamaica.

My Uncle Sidney was a competent lawyer and totally trustworthy financially and professionally. He was also a snob and a narrow-minded bore, quite incapable of seeing anyone's point of view but his own. The first time I went to dinner at his house, a week or two after arriving home. I was treated to a long lecture, interrupted only by loud comments upon niggers, a subject upon which he considered himself an authority.

It was hard to imagine, he told us, but he had heard of some "brown boy" buying a car. "If we don't watch out," he said, "niggers will soon be owning cars, if you please." He was sick of niggers who did not know their place. The decent ones were all right; he couldn't stand the impudent ones. Though even the decent ones were damned fools, and never did anything properly, and couldn't be relied upon.

I ached with embarrassment, because neither my Uncle Sidney nor anyone else at the table made the slightest attempt to keep their opinions or their voices down while the two black maids were waiting at table. I was soon to learn that this habit of downgrading and insulting the Negro race in general in the hearing of Negro servants was very widespread among Jamaican Whites. But the experience that night was new to me. I had never heard it happen at home. My father's views were little different essentially from those of his older brother, but he had better manners and was a more considerate man.

I was also too young to understand that the kind of prejudice that I was witnessing was a matter of psychopathology and not a matter of opinion amenable to argument or discussion. As black servants were strictly nonpeople in the eyes of men like my Uncle Sidney, it was not, to him, even a matter of ill manners to express such opinions in their hearing. He did not ill-treat his servants; he even had affection for some of them, but they stood exactly on a par with his Cocker spaniels, except that as the dogs were unable to answer back or make any claim to humanity, they at no time presented a challenge and never incurred my uncle's displeasure.

Eighteen-year-olds are seldom wise. Certainly I was not. Had I been wise I would have let the whole appalling dinner conversation go in through one ear and out the other as I concentrated on more pleasant thoughts of my own. But my embarrassment turned into anger. It had so happened that two days before I had driven to a little town called Linstead to visit Elizabeth Selvyn, who was in retirement on a pension from my father. It had been a joyful reunion with my old Nanny. The remarks at my uncle's dinner table seemed to me an affront to my beloved Elizabeth Selvyn in particular as well as a great deal of pernicious nonsense in general.

I said so.

My protest came, if I remember rightly, between the fish and the main course, which is the worst possible time to disrupt a dinner with abrasive opinions, and yet another proof of my eighteen-year-old lack of sophistication. I think it is a bad idea to disrupt dinner with a heated argument at any stage, for all it does is to spoil the food, and no person with acute indigestion is ever amenable to reason.

If you are going to disrupt dinner, it is sensible to wait until after the main course, so that if the stage of acrimony is reached where you have to get up and leave, at least you leave on a full belly.

When I came to the end of my protest, my uncle was purple with rage. He did not attempt to argue with me. He merely called me various versions of a damned ignorant young fool at some length. The whole thing was the stormy beginning of a long and unpleasant relationship for both of us.

I wondered then why the Blacks of Jamaica had not long ago arisen and slit the throats of their white masters, for they outnumbered the Whites twenty to one. No small English regiment, no matter how well armed, could have contained a large and determined uprising. I concluded at the time that the reason for it was that the Blacks were remarkably gentle, tolerant, and patient; but later I revised this view. Gentle, tolerant and patient they certainly were and are, but I came to understand that the barrage of belittlement to which the Negro was subjected, a belittlement not only directly symptomized by the kind of conversation which my Uncle Sidney and so many others seemed compelled to indulge in, but a belittlement indirectly but pervasively inflicted by the whole white colonial ambiance, was what in fact kept the Whites safe. It made the Negro doubt and despise himself; and people consumed with self-hatred have little time to spend upon hatred for others.

It is not until the Negro ceases to doubt or to hate himself that he can feel strongly about the people and the systems which have sought to rob him of his self-respect; which is why anti-white feeling becomes strong, not at the beginning of a process of liberation, but near its end when such feelings would, on the face of it seem no longer necessary or sensible.

My Uncle Sidney, were he alive today, would say that this was yet another example of the Negro habit of biting the hand that feeds him. But then my Uncle Sidney is not alive today; he died many years ago of a prostate disorder after managing to acquire five wives, one quasi-permanent mistress, and quite a lot of money, none of which, alas, he left to me.

But the historical events which created people like Uncle Sidney are not to be halted by individual deaths. Countries like Jamaica are synthetic. Virtually everything about Jamaica was the creation of the colonial power. The sugar cane plant which brought wealth to the estates was imported. Most of the estate owners were absentees and lived in England. The ancestors of everybody now called a Jamaican were imported. Even the main protein food for the slaves, salted cod, was imported. Jamaica was simply an estate put together for the convenience, the defense, and the enrichment of England; and those purposes were the sole reason for the island's existence as a going concern. When those purposes ceased to apply, there was really no point in the place continuing to exist at all.

But there the island was, stubbornly existing, beautiful, grossly overpopulated in relation to its resources, exceedingly poor. As a business Jamaica had ceased to make a profit. Like sensible businessmen, the English got rid of their liability in a hurry. They gave the place to their employees in place of gold watches for three hundred years of more or less faithful service. The ex-employees didn't know they had been fired. They thought they had skillfully won their right to take over the business. They never even asked for severance pay.

So isolated were they in their Caribbean backwater and so carefully conditioned, that they could only mumble the catch phrases of more-English-than-the-English loyalty on the one hand or London School of Economics parrot cries on the other. Both were irrelevant. So busy were people waving or desecrating the Union Jack that nobody saw the point, which was that had Jamaica declared that it intended to remain a British colony forever, Britain, desperate to be rid of it, would eventually have paid a very substantial settlement for a divorce. This, in turn, might have given us the basis of real economic independence instead of the sham independence for which we now claim we "fought" but which Britain dropped into our laps with a sigh of understandable relief.

So a mere colony without an identity of its own became a synthetic country with a synthetic independence, without a balance in the bank.

In 1834, when slavery had been abolished, the good men who had contrived the legal freedom of the slaves had given no thought to how those slaves were to continue to support themselves. In the first flush of freedom, the slaves had deserted the plantations and taken to the hills where they began quietly to starve. So they had to return to the plantations to work as free men for a money wage somewhat less than the value of the food and clothes they had received as slaves. The plantation owners received compensation from England for the loss of their slaves; so when things settled down, all that freedom for the slaves had done was to provide extra capital and cheaper labor for their masters.

One would have thought that this would have provided a lasting lesson for Jamaicans to the effect that political freedom means nothing without the economic reality of freedom. But it did not. One hundred and thirty years later the same mistake was made on a national scale. That moment of glory when in 1962 the Jamaican flag was hoisted, as the Union Jack came down, was the sickest joke yet in the Jamaican story.

In spite of all that, Jamaica came for a while within an inch or two of making itself a going concern. Then new management came along, production dropped and the new managers issued bogus shares and bogus prospectuses and printed the money for the dividends. So Jamaica went bust again. It is not possible to live a pleasant life on bogus promises and bogus rhetoric, with the inevitable consequences of restrictions, bitterness, and crime.

14

In 1937 I was admitted to practice as Solicitor of the Supreme Court of Judicature of Jamaica. It was a nice long title that did me no good whatsoever; for my relationship with my Uncle Sidney had grown so sour that I was determined to escape from his law office as soon as I could and give up the practice of law.

The opportunity to do so began with the arrival in Jamaica of a neat, diminutive man called Mortimer Spring, who was a vice-president either of Loew's or of MGM, I now forget which. For two or three years previous to Mortimer Spring's arrival no MGM or 20th Century-Fox films had been shown in Jamaica. The reason for this was that the Jamaican company which had the monopoly of the film exhibition business had considered the price asked for MGM and 20th Century-Fox films to be far too high, and refused to pay it. MGM realized that if their films were ever to be shown in Jamaica either the price would have to be reduced or the theatre monopoly would have to be broken.

The MGM people decided upon the latter course. They persuaded a client of my father's, a wealthy man called B. M. Andrade, to put up the money for the building of a large luxury cinema in Kingston which would get the exclusive rights to the exhibition of MGM and 20th Century-Fox films.

B. M. Andrade in his turn came to my father to advise him on the negotiations. In due course a splendid, modern cinema, called the Carib, the first large building in the West Indies to be air-conditioned, was built. MGM and 20th Century-Fox films began to flow once more into Jamaica. But this did not come about without generating large amounts of bad blood on all sides.

It was all a beautiful little small-town brawl. Audley Morais, the managing director of the old monopoly, the Palace Amusement Company, was no longer speaking to B. M. Andrade. It was being put about that the inevitable result of entering an air-conditioned cinema was a terminal attack of pneumonia.

In this atmosphere of intense and emotional competition, the assorted motion picture distributors began jacking up the prices of their products to both sides. Mr. Mortimer Spring was as happy as a lark. He went back to his office in New York, stared appreciatively at his own reflection in his polished shoes, and bought himself an extra large cigar. He had made Jamaica safe for Metro-Goldwyn-Mayer.

At this point the Cinema Company of Jamaica, the company which had been formed to build and operate the Carib, found itself in need of a general manager. My father, knowing that I was unhappy at his office, arranged for me to take the job.

There must be problems in common with the running of large cinemas everywhere, but Jamaica seemed to present a few special mysteries. There was, for example, one small mystery I never solved. People were always leaving things on or under their seats. We used to collect them and put them up carefully. In time, most of the things, such as spectacles, pens, lipsticks and wallets, were called for by their owners.

One morning we found, under four adjacent seats, a pair of ladies' panties, an unused condom, an unspent revolver bullet, and a wedding ring (not engraved) in that order. I put all these objects away carefully, my imagination racing to compose a story which would logically account for my discoveries. I am convinced that there must have been some drama behind it all. I never found out. Nobody ever called for any of the items.

There was, however, at least one mystery we did solve, though not perhaps in the best way. In 1939, long before public indiscipline and vandalism became a normal part of life, I couldn't understand why a toilet seat in our ladies' room was found cracked in half nearly every Sunday morning. In those days, toilet seats were made of wood—the kind made of molded plastics not yet having been invented. One didn't have to be a genius to surmise that something was happening on Saturday nights to cause the breakage, but the question was, what? My directors, faced with almost weekly bills for new toilet seats, were demanding an explanation. B. M. Andrade, our Chairman and majority shareholder, who was notoriously mean, had begun to infer that in some sinister way I was aiding and abetting the flow of some of his profits down the drain.

My chief projectionist at the time was a charming but rather eccentric young man called Kerrith Saunders, who was later to become a pilot in the RAF and, after World War II, Jamaica's Deputy Director of Civil Aviation. He tended toward logical, if radical, solutions to problems.

I called Kerrith in to discuss the problem of the toilet seat. We had a few girls employed at the Carib as ushers and ticket sellers, and we asked them if any of them were prepared to sit in the ladies' room on Saturday nights to keep an eye on things. They all rather unreasonably refused. Kerrith then said that he would do this in drag, but one careful look at Kerrith, with his hairy chest, rugged features, and knobby knees, convinced me that such a scheme would be disastrous.

We finally decided on another course. There was a high, narrow window in the ladies' room which commanded a splendid view of all operations. It looked out over the parking lot at the back, and because of the difference in levels the sill was a good fifteen feet above the tarmac. Kerrith, we decided, would stand on a ten-foot stepladder we had in the office and keep watch through the window. Kerrith was delighted at the prospect of an evening show which he would not be projecting.

B. M. Andrade had a large number of relatives, among whom was a widow called Mrs. Solas. Mrs. Solas was a lady of enormous size. She had a fifteen-year-old son who was also of gigantic proportions. It had something to do with their glands, for Mrs. Solas's mother, long dead of a heart attack, had also been enormous. They were not merely fat, their obesity was mountainous. B. M. Andrade was much attached to Mrs. Solas. So much so that in spite of his meanness, I had been instructed to issue mother and son a free pass to the Carib. I had also adapted seats for them by removing the armrests from two seats so that they had four to sit on between them.

Saturday night came and Kerrith took up his position on the top of the stepladder. He had been perching there for two hours when Mrs. Solas entered the ladies' room and began the complicated logistical undertaking of getting herself, with much grunting and hard breathing, upon the seat.

Kerrith was fascinated. He gripped the windowsill and pulled himself up from the top of the stepladder in order to get a better view. Mrs. Solas, now suitably unencumbered by sundry undergarments, sat heavily down upon the seat, which promptly disintegrated with a loud crack. At which point Mrs. Solas happened to look up, saw a head at the window, and started to scream. Kerrith dodged down quickly, but lost his foothold on the stepladder, and he and the ladder crashed ten feet to the tarmac of the parking lot below.

The whole thing became a shambles. Fortunately, Mrs. Solas had not recognized Kerrith and in her indignant report to her relation, the Chairman, she spoke only of seeing the head "of a criminal assailant" staring at her through the window. She did not, at any time, mention the breaking of the toilet seat. She was far too self-conscious about her weight.

I had solved the mystery, but it did me little good with the directors, for I could not say that Mrs. Solas had been responsible without admitting that Kerrith had been spying upon her, and this was out of the question. The police held an inquiry about the "criminal assailant" but got nowhere because I had bought the silence of the car-park attendant with two bottles of white rum and the promise of more.

One good thing came out of it. Mrs. Solas never again used our ladies' room, and I never again had a broken toilet seat.

I wasn't managing the Carib for long before I came to the fairly obvious conclusion that the intense competition between the Cinema Company of Jamaica and The Palace Amusement Company was doing no one any good except the film salesmen. The obvious thing to do was for the two companies to amalgamate, restore the monopoly position, and give Mr. Mortimer Spring and the rest of them a screwing. The

Carib, having been built at enormous cost, left no possibility that anyone else would be interested in setting up yet another competing cinema.

The difficulty was that a lot of personal enmities and small-town rivalries had been created. To get B. M. Andrade to the same table as Audley Morais without having to call out the riot squad seemed virtually impossible. But there is one good thing about the rich: you can always rely upon their enthusiasm for a profit to overcome their dedication to an ideal.

So in the end, in the interests of the profit-and-loss account, Audley Morais and B. M. Andrade got together, dragging their assorted satellites with them, into a merger which made the two rivals one. I was given a new job—that of Advertising Manager for the merged concern. I met a man called Herbert Hart, then the Assistant Manager of The Palace Amusement Company, a meeting which was the beginning of a valued and lasting friendship. We converted a number of seats in a number of cinemas to encompass the behinds of Solas *Mère et Fils,* and nearly everyone lived happily, if not forever after, at least for a few years.

15

During those few years, Herbert Hart and I became rather bored with living in Jamaica. It is a little difficult to say why. The Jamaica of the tourist brochures, the Paradise Island with blue mountains and white sands, and a climate which must be as near to perfection as it is possible to get, is true enough as far as it goes, but it only goes as far as its upper classes or its visitors.

I was born a member of the old plantocracy. In addition to our big, rambling house in Kingston, we had a beautiful house in the blue mountains 4,000 feet above sea level, where we went to avoid the heat of the plains in summer. I spent much of my childhood on my uncles' sugar estates in Westmoreland, in lovely mahogany-and-stone Great Houses, where we could ride on our own land, swim and fish in our own rivers and on our own beaches, and go on private alligator hunts in the cool pewter dawns of Jamaica. We had servants to look after us, to wash for us—even to pick and to roast the breadfruit on campfires made up on the beach as we swam.

We were not lotus eaters. My father and my uncles worked hard. My uncles rose at dawn on a working day and rode their estates, and they were tough men who could turn their hands to most tasks, including delivering the babies of their female workers if necessary. None of us was brought up "soft." At the age of eleven, I was given a twelve-bore shotgun and told how to use it. And when, on my first try, it kicked me flat—for they had not told me that it was double-choked—I was made to get up and try again immediately until I mastered it.

Nor were we simply backwoodsmen. In general, the middle classes in Jamaica were cut off from much that was going on in the world outside. At parties given by the colonial administrators and attended by the newly rich entrepreneurs and by some of the more Neanderthal planters, the conversation was exceptionally tedious.

George Orwell in *Burmese Days* paints a cruel but accurate picture of conversation at "the Club" which must have been standard at that time not only in Burma but throughout the entire British Colonial Empire whenever three or four Whites or their emulators gathered together to bemoan the perfidy of the "natives." Yet Jamaica always had a dimension which so many other outposts lacked. That was a small minority of people whose intellectual accomplishments and breadth of vision were of the highest order.

This was possibly because of a large influx of Sephardic Jews, and because many members of the old plantocracy had the leisure and the money to acquire admirable educations and to travel extensively. These were the exceptions. At my uncles' plantations the conversation was good and the wit sharp. It is easier to spend the time polishing one's aphorisms if there are servants to polish one's silver.

We lived in our own world, waited on hand and foot by others. It occurred to few of us that this was not the normal, natural order of things.

There had to be another side, and it was this side of Jamaica which made our side of it possible, and to which the visitor seldom penetrated. It was the side of the little wattle-and-daub huts or, much worse, the shabby shanties which looked as if they had been made out of old packing cases and rusty corrugated iron. It was the side of the men and women working on the land for sixpence a day; black men and women cut away from their roots by slavery and freed to live in penury. Any attempt by them to retain their own customs or their own forms of worship was outlawed. The majority of people lived at subsistence level to serve a minority of masters.

Of course, it was a pattern old as the hills. It wasn't uniquely Jamaican. It had been the same in Russia, in France, in England. But there were two things which added an extra dimension. In Jamaica the serf was a "nigger." God had branded him forever. Secondly, the date was important. It was the 1930s. The pattern, at one time accepted, had long outlived its time. The social pattern in the Jamaica of, say, 1937, was as anomalous as a picture showing Cleopatra calling Caesar up on the telephone.

That was the trouble with Jamaica at most levels. Every accepted idea, every accepted attitude in Jamaica, was at least fifty years displaced in time. To this day, the people tend to be like flies encased in amber. In 1950 I used to wonder when some heated discussion would not break out in the press as to whether the use of anesthetics in childbirth was against the laws of God. While life in Jamaica for the upper classes was easy and pleasant on the physical level, it was, in 1935, just about the most boring place to be if one was interested in ideas. There wasn't a bookshop, properly so called, on the entire island.

Among many of the planters, newly promoted from overseers to ownership, there was a determined cult of low-browism; of loud and often drunken behavior in public places. They were rednecks with all the trappings of a ruling class, but without the sensitivity, the intelligence, or the knowledge to discharge their obligations. Many were semi-literate. I knew two very rich ones whose only exercise of the art of writing was to sign checks; and even this they barely managed. Their brown-skinned counterparts, their "social inferiors" until they became very rich, developed their own brand of very special vulgarity—a vulgarity which until this day sets the tone of what, I suppose, one may call Jamaican society.

People wrote and talked in clichés borrowed from other cultures, so it was not surprising that they usually used them wrongly or subtly out-of-meaning, giving a weird flavor to public speeches or letters to the press. Somebody once described the island of Jamaica as a cemetery of dead metaphors. It should be added that they were buried only after having been tortured to death; and the corpses, zombie-like, still roam the country.

I am sure that Sheridan's Mrs. Malaprop must have been based upon a Jamaican lady. One old planter I knew told me on various occasions that he intended to plant a revénue of populous trees and to import a hydraulic ram to improve the breed of his sheep. On one trip abroad, the old man and his wife went to Italy. Recounting their experiences the wife said that they had been most disappointed in the Bridge of Sighs.

"Why?" someone asked.

"Well," said the old man, "it's not of any size at all."

These people were not just rough frontiersmen, unlettered but redeemed by work, courage and faith. They were people pampered and spoiled by slavery and its aftermath, social usurpers lost in a cultural Limbo, held aloft by the "niggers" they spurned. It is needless to say that there were many exceptions; there always are. But the exceptions merely served to prove the rule of the vulgar and the third-rate; people without ideas or idealisms even more corrupted by slavery than the slaves themselves.

Herbert Hart had taken a degree in electrical engineering at McGill, but there was no opportunity for him to practice his profession. When in 1939 war was declared, we decided that this provided as useful an opportunity as any to make good our escape from our Colonial outpost. But we soon found that there was no means by which we could volunteer for service. Hitler had made some remark to the effect that the British intended to die to the last colonial, and this had made the English edgy.

In any event, this was the period of the phony war when Britain and France thought they could just sit safely behind the Maginot Line until the German armies died of frustration, and we were told that what England needed was dollars, not men. My wife, too, needed a bit of persuasion to leave Jamaica. She also was bored with the place but, like so many women, she had an oyster complex: wherever you put her down, she wanted to stay.

So Herbert went first in 1940 at his own expense on a banana boat. We followed in 1941. We found Herbert in a cheap hotel in Notting Hill Gate, all his socks in holes, and in a room so small that you couldn't open the door fully without moving the bed. Because of his considerable qualifications and ability, they had refused to put him into the armed forces but had sent him to the Ministry of Aircraft Production where he had been grabbed for a most responsible job.

Herbert had calculated that the pay of an English private soldier amounted to three pounds, fifteen shillings and sixpence a week. He refused, therefore, to accept more than this as his salary—an eccentricity that had thrown the entire Establishment's division of the Ministry of Aircraft Production into confusion for weeks. But the problem had somehow been solved and Herbert had won, with the consequence that he was in an abject state of poverty and was extremely happy. Herbert Hart is the kind of man who is at his happiest when he's miserable.

Barbara soon got a war job at modest pay, and I ended up doing a weekly broadcast for the BBC and being employed as Business Manager of the Crown Film Unit at Pinewood, which was producing documentaries for the war effort. All three of us moved into a rather squalid flat in Earls Court and Barbara darned some of Herbert's socks. So our war began.

None of us spilled a drop of blood in anger. Herbert was soon made an air raid warden, which meant that in the evening after he came home from work, he had to get into his uniform and his tin hat and help clear up the mess after an air raid. His beat happened to be an area which included a large graveyard. Though he did spend a few bad nights shoveling corpses into graves after the bombs fell, he never had a corpse that was fresher than 1937.

My war began in earnest when I arrived for my first day at the huge Pinewood film studio in Buckingham. The studio workers were on strike and had been on strike for some weeks. A young woman introduced herself to me as my secretary. She was very shapely, very sexy, and very smartly dressed. She carried a notebook and a pencil in her hand. She told me her name was Livia. My delight at the prospect of having Livia around was soon dimmed, however, when I discovered that she could neither type nor do shorthand. She was just seventeen years old. I asked her why, in that case, she carried a notebook and a pencil, and why she constantly followed me around wherever I went, for she would trot along about three paces behind me—notebook and pencil at the ready. She said that was how she'd seen secretaries in the movies behave.

Though it was difficult to get away from Livia, who stuck to me with the persistence of a bloodhound, I managed to shake her long enough to put through a call to the Ministry of Information near Russell Square.

"Look here." I said to the man who answered. "I am Cargill, the new business manager of the Crown Film Unit. You've assigned me a secretary named Livia. She's gorgeous and all that, but she can't type. She can't do shorthand. She has never had a job before. What do you expect me to do with her?"

"Don't be so ratty, old chap," the man said, "do anything you like so long of course as it's not on government time."

"Be serious." I said. "How the hell can I do my work without a proper secretary? This one just keeps following me around, and she's driving me mad!"

"Don't you know there's a war on, my dear fellow? We just can't get secretaries."

"Well, you've managed to get Livia."

"Oh, she was a special case."

"How do you mean—a special case?"

"Well, they tell me she is Joe Loss's vocalist. And these big name bands don't want to lose their singers to the ATS and so on. So they put them on ice at the Ministry of Information."

"Marvelous." I said. "I'll get her to sing to me. In the meantime, though, if you expect any of your endless fucking memos to be replied to, you'd better find me a real secretary."

"Come now, Cargill," the man said. "Let us not descend to obscenities." And he hung up.

I've got to admit, though, that Livia was a resourceful girl. She knew all the studio gossip and was a mine of backstairs information. I learned from her on my second day that the real cause of the strike was a Communist shop steward. Russia had not yet come into the war against Germany, so the war's instant transformation from a capitalist-imperialist adventure into a war of worker liberation had not yet taken place. I told Livia to go and find the shop steward and tell him I wanted to see him.

Livia shortly returned, followed by a tall, bearded man of about my own age. He had so much hair on his face that all I could see were two rather close-together eyes and a long nose. He wore a red shirt and corduroy trousers and sandals.

"Do sit down." I said, offering him a chair.

"I'd rather stand if yer don't moind," he replied.

"I am told that you are all on strike," I said. "Can I be of any help in settling the matter?"

"Well, it ain't an official strike. The trade union bosses have sold out to the capitalists."

"So this is just a kind of wildcat affair?"

"Yes, I suppose you could call it that."

"Well, what's your grievance? Has it to do with pay and conditions?"

"O'il be frank with you," he replied. "Under capitalist oppression all pay and conditions are bad. But as far as that goes, we are getting the right rates."

"Then why are you on strike?"

"Because this is a capitalist war. 'Itler and our lot are all the syme. The workers must take no part in it."

"But your country is at war," I said.

"Aw, don't give me that patriotic shit," he said. "That kind of thing is only used to pull the wool over the workers' eyes."

"Do all the people on the floor think as you do?"

"They do what I tell 'em."

"Look," I said. "My job is to get this place back to work. You will, I am sure, understand my position. I am going to do it even if it means appealing to people over your head or firing you and the whole bloody lot."

"Yer don't seem to realize that we are now established civil servants. Yer can't do it."

"I can, you know. And I will."

"You would say that. You are just another of them la-de-da capitalist lackeys who will have to be swept away comes the revolution."

"The revolution hasn't come yet. Until that blessed day comes you are going to go back to work."

"Look 'ere, mate," said the shop steward belligerently. "Are you threatening me? If you think I'm going to take that from the likes of you, you got another thought coming. I don't like your type. All you think about is the oppression of the masses."

I had had enough. I figured it was time he experienced a bit of real oppression. I was twenty-six, quick-tempered, and quite inexperienced in these matters. I got up, took careful aim, and hit him—a nice, fat right on the nose. His head jerked back, and he collapsed onto the floor with a surprised expression on his face. His nose started to bleed copiously.

I said, "Now get out! Unless, of course, you want me to knock your bloody brains out."

He pulled himself up from the floor, clutching his nose, took one frightened look at me, and fled.

Livia, who had been the inevitable witness to all this, was delighted. She was clapping her hands.

"It was just like a scene from a movie I saw the other day!" she said.

I turned to Livia. "I shouldn't have done that, of course. All hell will probably now break loose."

"Nobody can blame you for *defending* yourself," she observed, her face now expressionless.

"But I wasn't defending myself, Livia."

"Oh, yes, you were. I saw when he rushed you, and you had to hit him to protect yourself." Her face was like a mask. "And me," she added, "he could have raped me, you know, if you had been lying senseless on the floor after his vicious attack."

Livia was clearly living again all the B-movies she'd ever seen.

So it was that Livia and I framed the shop steward. With every retelling, Livia's story became more dramatic and more steamy, and in the end everyone regarded the unfortunate shop steward not only as an aggressor, but as a kind of sex maniac. The men all went back to work; the shop steward left —his nose in terrible shape—and everyone wanted to hear the story firsthand from Livia if only as an excuse for chatting her up.

Soon after this, one of our leading producers came to me. He undulated through the door. "Darling," he said, "I want to burn down that dreadful old barn we have."

"Why?"

"To make a scene for my film, of course."

"Well, why don't you?"

"Well, of course, darling, I couldn't do it without your permission. Besides, what are we going to do with all those sheep?"

"What sheep?" I asked.

"My goodness! Don't you know we have all those frightful sheep?"

I didn't, but I soon found out. Livia looked up the files and found that we had a large field and a barn, three hundred sheep and two shepherds. It was costing a fortune to feed the sheep—to say nothing of the salaries of the shepherds. I could find nothing on the file to say where the sheep had come from or why we owned them. I assigned Livia the task of getting me some background information.

A few days later, Livia said, "About those sheep. We have

had them for years. All I could find out is we inherited them from the Post Office Film Unit. They have been breeding a lot. Don't you think we could sell them?"

"We are part of the Civil Service," I told Livia, "and we just can't sell things like that. Get me the Ministry of Agriculture and Fisheries on the phone and ask for the department that does sheep."

It took a long time to get the right department, but finally the man in charge of sheep said, "We treat sheep for assorted diseases, and we help in the breeding and distribution of sheep, but we don't buy them or keep them. Sorry we can't be of help, my dear chap. You will just have to learn to live with your sheep, I'm afraid."

Livia next got the Post Office on the phone. I asked to speak to the Postmaster General, but that was too elevated an objective. The highest I could go was his deputy. Fortunately, the deputy knew about the sheep. He said, "My dear Cargill, you have come in on a long story. Many years ago the Post Office Film Unit, which your chaps took over, wanted three pairs of sheep for a documentary it was then making. This caused a lot of flap. You see, the Postmaster General did not have the power in law to acquire sheep. The Min. of Ag. couldn't either so we finally got around the problem by having the King buy them. We didn't actually talk to His Majesty, of course. We had a chap at the palace do the job."

"The trouble was," he went on, "we couldn't get rid of them after we were finished making the film, because the sheep are Crown property—like swans and deer and whales and all that—and the complications were enormous. So, we just kept them and they went on breeding and now you've got them. The only thing I can suggest is that you phone Buck House. Perhaps someone there could help you."

So I phoned Buckingham Palace. A very snooty fellow answered, and I told him my story. "You must be joking," he said.

"I am not, I assure you. What am I supposed to do with three hundred sheep? I just want permission to sell them."

"My dear fellow, I don't think you understand what is involved in the sale of Crown property."

"No, but I'm beginning to learn."

"Don't you know there's a war on?"

"Yes, someone told me."

"There's no point in being funny. The whole thing is out of the question. Goodbye."

I put down the telephone and turned to Livia. "It's no good," I said, "We are stuck with the sheep."

"I'll find a way out," said Livia. "You just leave it to me."

The next day, Livia was not in my office when I arrived. She came in two hours late, trailed by a middle-aged, plump little man in a blue suit and a bowler hat, carrying a black leather attaché case.

"I would like to introduce you to Mr. Peabody," she said to me. "He is the leading butcher in Chalfont-St.-Giles. I have spoken to him about the sheep."

"Your assistant here," said Mr. Peabody after we had shaken hands and he was seated, "has been kind enough to sell me three hundred sheep, Mr. Cargill. And I am most grateful to her—most grateful. As you must know, in these days of rationing and shortages, three hundred sheep will keep us going very nicely. I realize, of course, that this is what is frankly called a black market transaction, but you may rely utterly on my discretion."

I was paralyzed.

I was trying to think of something to say when Livia said brightly, "I told Mr. Peabody that you wanted three thousand pounds in used one-pound notes."

Mr. Peabody said, "Yes, indeed, they are all here in this bag, Mr. Cargill. I will leave the bag on your desk. I will be responsible for the removal of the sheep."

Livia got up. "Well, Mr. P.," she said, "that's it. It was nice of you to help us."

Before I could utter a word, she ushered Mr. Peabody out of the room.

When she came back, she was smiling broadly and said, "Now aren't I a clever girl?"

"Yes, Livia," I said.

"I saw a movie once where they always got old used notes for things like this, so they can't trace the serial numbers."

"Yes, Livia," I said again.

"And we're going to have a lovely time spending that money—aren't we?"

I thought the time had come to assert myself.

"No, Livia," I said firmly. "That money does not belong to us. It belongs to the Crown. You have already broken at least three laws, for which we could rot in prison for ages. I am not adding larceny to our offenses."

"Oh, my," said Livia, crestfallen. "Are you angry?"

"No, I am not angry, Livia, I said, "only terrified. Now I am going straight to London to deposit that bag with their Lordships of the Treasury."

"You won't tell on me, will you?"

"No, of course not."

"What will you say?"

"I haven't the faintest idea."

"Oh, my," said Livia again, looking longingly at the black bag as I picked it up and left.

Their Lordships of the Treasury, in the form of a pale, bespectacled Civil Servant called Beauchamp, were horrified. It was not so much at the immorality or illegality of the transaction, but at the fact that there was no way in which the file could be gotten "right."

"There is no authorization for this transaction," he said. "Have you any memos in support?"

"No." I said, "I just sold the bloody sheep. Here is the

money. It belongs to the Crown. Give it to the Crown. God knows the Crown needs the money to buy rifles and things. Don't you know," I added, thinking of my snooty Buckingham Palace chum, "there's a war on?"

"You are rocking the boat, you know, Cargill," said the representative of their Lordships as I left.

God knows what happened to the money. Come to think of it, I should have taken Livia's advice, but I was young then and starry-eyed, and, God preserve me, believed in doing the "right" thing.

The establishment's Division of the Ministry of Information soon transferred Livia and sent me a real secretary. When the time came for Livia to leave, I was truly sorry to see her go, and she was in tears. I don't think the tears went very deep. I'm sure she shed them because she had seen it happen in a movie, for her entire life was governed by screen clichés.

Before she went she rendered me one more great service. She had, she told me, an aunt who was a nun. This nun, she said, had a number of clothing coupons which she had no use for, and she would get them for me if I wanted them.

I certainly did. I had arrived in England in midwinter with no winter clothing and no means of getting any, for the clothing ration was very small. So Livia brought me her aunt's coupons, half a year's supply of them, and I rushed to Austin Reed's and bought myself warm underclothes. I often wondered whether the government ever checked to see what people did with their coupons and, if they did, what they made of a nun who bought male underclothing at Austin Reed's.

The temporary civil servants, of whom I was one, who were brought in during the war to help man the new and extended government departments, were a sore trial to the permanents. Being, to use a phrase of John O'Connor Power, like mules, without pride of ancestry or hope of posterity, the temporaries were apt to break all the rules when it suited them. Unlike the permanents, whose careers depended upon their having no black marks against them in the files, the temporaries could not have cared less. They spent money without treasury authorization when a job had to be done in a hurry, and let their Lordships worry about a sin which would have put an end to a permanent's hope of promotion. The temporaries, when necessary, did not bother about what was called "the usual channels"; they went over people's heads when this got them what they wanted.

I don't think the civil service could be run like this in peacetime, but it had its advantages during a war. It also had other advantages. It loosened up the whole system and made a great deal of sport with civil service jargon, effects which lasted long after the temporaries had gone.

I was astonished, when I first joined the Ministry of Information, to discover how the permanents handled the simplest matters. A member of the public, say, or another ministry, would write in about something or another. The permanent civil servant in whose "in" tray the letter would be placed would then write a memo, "calling for the file" which would arrive two days later, carried by a messenger and again put in his "in" tray, with the letter pinned to the cover.

The study of the file would take some days. Then the civil servant would write a reply to the letter in his own hand, mark it "draft please," and put it in his "out" tray. In due course the messenger would carry it to the typing pool, and after a day or two more, the typed draft would arrive back in the "in" tray.

At this point, the really laborious business began. The civil servant would then pin the draft reply to the letter and pin both to the file. These would be directed to the head of his department with a memo something like this:

> Please see letter dated August 1st from General Hardware Ltd. of Birmingham, complaining about the shortage

> of chamber pots. It is possible that this is a matter which comes within the purview of our department, as it is a matter which could be said to concern civilian morale (See Ministry Paper 15, Para. 5, Subpara. 2, dated 16th June). Your views please. In the meantime, I propose we contact the Ministry of Trade, the Ministry of Supply and the Ministry of Labour, as their views may be essential. Do you agree?

A month would then pass. Eventually, the file would return, with a number of memos showing that the file had ultimately reached the Minister himself, and had once more come down to earth. The Principal's memo would read:

> Please see Minister's views with which I concur. Your noncommittal draft reply is admirable except for changing "the" to "those" in the first paragraph and "sit" to "be seated" in the second paragraph in order to avoid any possibility of a typographical error. Suggest you now pass the buck to the three Ministries mentioned.

Having got his authority, the civil servant would send the amended draft reply back to the typing pool for engrossment. The reply would reach the firm some two months after its letter had been written.

Another thing I learned was that the furniture in one's room, down to the last detail, depended upon one's rank. Those below the rank of Assistant Principal had desks with plain wooden tops. With the rank of Assistant Principal, the top began to grow a small square of green baize. The hatrack hanging behind the door also sprouted another prong. With the rank of Principal, the green baize grew to cover nearly half the desk, and the hatrack, now with four prongs, no longer hung behind the door but stood with dignity on its own feet. Only Ministers or an Undersecretary of State had desks entirely covered with green baize or were entitled to a personal secretary.

The temporaries soon changed all that. They got themselves decent desks, useful hatracks, personal secretaries. They substituted the telephone for a good deal of memo-writing, and strolled into the office of their superiors to get instant decisions. They replied to letters and took a lot of action on their own authority and sometimes fouled things up terribly. But they also got a lot of useful work done in a hurry.

Sometimes it was not possible to beat the system. On one occasion, an electric light bulb in my office blew. I was caught red-handed by the messenger standing on my desk putting a new one in. This created a monstrous row with the trade union involved and the Ministry of Works, both of whom shared the monopoly of replacing blown light bulbs in government offices. I settled the row by apologizing, and arranging for a workman and his mate, complete with a step-ladder, to come and unscrew my bulb, and screw it back in again.

The temporaries also had mild fun with their memo-writing. On one occasion, one of them received a file with a long memo from a permanent civil servant. Having read it, he was poising his pen to write the simple word "Balls" beneath it, when he became overcome with unusual prudence, and instead wrote "Round Objects."

The file went on its usual travels, and when it eventually returned he found out that our Minister, who was at that time Brendan Bracken, had written deadpan beneath it, in his neat hand, "Who is Mr. Round? And why does he object?"

16

After I was moved up to Russell Square from Pinewood Studios, I was enlisted into the Home Guard, 2nd City of London Battalion. Dad's Army, comprised largely of the old, the halt, and the lame, armed with World War I bolt-action rifles, Sten guns and grenade throwers, were expected to throw themselves upon the enemy in the event of an invasion of England. I have an idea that this gallant band would have been far more dangerous to themselves than to the Germans.

One of the things that appealed to me about our Ministry Home Guard was that our headquarters was way down in the basement under the tall, modern, steel-and-concrete building of the University of London, which had been taken over by the Ministry of Information for the duration of the war. It was quite the safest place in London to be in during an air raid.

Herbert Hart and my first wife had early decided never to go to a shelter during an air raid, and to ignore falling bombs with an aristocratic disdain. I could hardly do anything but to emulate them, though my heart wasn't in it and my knees never ceased dissolving into jelly when the bombs started to fall nearby.

They carried the business to what seemed to me an unnecessary length. One night in our rather squalid apartment in Earls Court we were playing gin rummy when the sirens went. The bombs began to fall nearer and nearer with their usual nasty thumps, and I knew that the German bombers were pretty well right overhead when "our" anti-aircraft gun began barking like an angry giant dog. As usual, Barbara and Herbert paid no attention at all. Suddenly, I noticed that the room was filling with smoke.

I said, "I think there's a bit of smoke about," not wishing to seem too concerned.

"Oh, it's nothing," said Herbert. "Probably just from a burning building nearby.

"Go on with the game," Barbara said.

The smoke got thicker and thicker. My eyes began to smart. The smell was most alarming. Even Herbert began to wipe his eyes. I was just about to say very firmly that I didn't give a damn about their stiff upper lips, but that I was getting the hell out, when there was a loud banging on the front door, and when I opened it two very irate air raid wardens in tin hats came barging in.

"You are showing a chink of light through the curtain," said one. "Don't you know there is a raid on?"

The other one took a great sniff. "Great God!" he said. "Where's all the smoke coming from?"

"Here," said the first. "Don't you know your bloody wastepaper basket's on fire?"

So it was. It had, by this time, more or less burnt itself out to a pile of ashes, basket and all. What was worse, it had burnt a nasty great hole in our landlady's carpet. The wardens stamped out the remaining embers and departed, muttering under their breaths.

"You must have thrown a lighted cigarette into the basket," Herbert said accusingly, peering at me as best he could through the smoke.

"Now I come to think of it, I did," I admitted. "But if you two hadn't been so damned imperturbable, we might have discovered it earlier."

"Oh well, never mind," said Barbara. "It could have been worse. It could have been an incendiary."

"That carpet is going to cost us a month's pay," Herbert said. "It wouldn't have cost us anything if it had been an incendiary."

"Well, what do you expect me to do?" I asked. "Go out and signal to the Luftwaffe to drop one on us? Besides," I added, "if only you'd stop refusing to take more than three pounds, fifteen shillings and sixpence a week, we'd be able to pay for it sooner."

The smoke soon cleared. The all-clear went, and we went back to the game of rummy. In the morning we would need our energies to face the landlady.

So it was a luxury for me to have a nice deep shelter to go to once a week with the face-saving excuse that I was a soldier obeying orders.

I joined the Home Guard as a private. My uniform was quite remarkably ill-fitting, and the brass buttons seemed stubbornly shine-resistant. One of the things I discovered almost immediately was how to get out of polishing my buttons. Our sergeant, who was a great stickler for spit-and-polish, and who had an old soldier's unfailing instinct for spotting any cheating like varnished buttons, happened to be the office messenger in my division at the Ministry. I was happily in the position of making life easier for him in sundry minor ways. We made a pact. I wouldn't notice if he turned up late for work or went home a bit early, and in return he would polish my buttons and clean my boots. He couldn't do anything about my ill-fitting uniform, but my buttons shone like stars and were the envy of all.

My peace and quiet as a private was soon shattered. Many things contributed to this. First of all, the major in command of our section was a friend of mine, a delightful man called Harley Usill. He took his part-time military duties very seriously and was exceedingly gung-ho about them. He kept nagging me to the effect that as I had been to a leading English public school and had gone through the officer's training course and all that, it was letting down the side not becoming an officer. He regarded my military slumming as almost a personal affront.

I had kept on ignoring his entreaties partly because as a private I had the company of the most interesting people, including a retired admiral, two psychiatrists (one of whom said he suffered from chronic anxiety), a doctor, a lawyer and a remarkably talented financier who ended up, I regret to say, in jail. Partly, too, I felt that I really wasn't cut out for the military life and would make a very inadequate officer.

Between us, Barbara and I happened to have two relatives who were distinguished generals; Frank Nosworthy on my side and Mickey Rodwell on hers. We had been staying the weekend with Mickey and his wife Nell. Mickey was then in command of southern England, and he had asked me if I would find it interesting to accompany him on a tour of inspection.

"I'm going next Saturday," he said. "Wear your uniform. You can come as my adjutant."

I knew that he knew I was in the Home Guard. I also

knew that he had never for a moment considered that I might not be an officer. So I broke the news to him that I had an evilly-fitting uniform, and that I was a private.

"Well, in that case," Mickey said, "you'd have to come as my batman, and we can't have that, can we?"

Frank Nosworthy also discovered my lowly rank.

"It's not that I'm against people joining up in the ranks," he said, rather red in the face. "The private soldier is the salt of the earth. He dies for our mistakes. But damn it, Morris, think of the family. Even mad old Cargill's a colonel, even if it's only in the sappers, and all he's ever done is to quarrel with the Astronomer Royal and write a lot of tripe about relativity.

So eventually I told my friend Harley that I was prepared to become an officer.

Before I could leap on the ladder of swift promotion, however, I had to pass a thing called the proficiency test. I nearly lost my life learning to throw hand grenades, for an old gentleman on my right with a rheumatic shoulder threw his first one a short distance straight up, and it dropped at our feet. Only the rapid reflexes of the sergeant-instructor saved us. He leapt for it, and threw it over the wall a split second before it exploded.

The rest of the course was fairly easy, except map-reading. I am one of those people who never know where North is. Or South, for that matter, or even East or West. I can lose my way in a small village. It took me a long time to learn to make any sense at all of a map. I pitied any group of men who might at some future time find themselves under my command. I was certain that I would lead them in an unfortunately wrong direction.

Nevertheless, the great day dawned when I was able to display upon the arm of my uniform the red star which signified I had passed my proficiency test. Harley was proud and delighted. I even let one of my "general" relatives understand that I would soon be an officer and a gentleman and would no longer disgrace them. Everything was all set for my rapid promotion.

The day after I got my red star, we received orders to turn out for a large parade, to be officially inspected by a certain well-known general, no relation. We were all standing to attention in long lines on the parade ground where I caught my first glimpse of the old bastard, and felt a sharp chill of foreboding, a kind of nameless fear of impending disaster. This general had the yellow-brownish skin, the bags under his eyes, and the intensely disagreeable expression which comes from long service in India, the habit of drinking too many pink gins, taking too many quinine tablets, and kicking too many sepoys.

As he walked down the ranks, on an inspection which, after all, was only meant as a formality, he came to a dead stop in front of me. He stared at me intently, up and down. Then he put out a hand and seized the neck of my tunic.

"God damn it, man. The thing doesn't fit. I can see clear down to your navel. Get this man," he said, turning to the officer behind him, "a better fitting uniform."

Then with one more venomous glance at me, as if I had been responsible for making my terrible garment, he passed on.

A bit of time passed, and I was wondering how much longer I would have to stand to attention, not daring to look either to left or right, when suddenly I felt someone grip the seat of my trousers from behind. It was the General passing between ranks. He shouted, "God blast you, sir. Your crotch is hanging down to your knees."

To this day, I am proud of the fact that I never moved.

We kept on standing to attention. Just as I thought that we would soon be getting some relief, for one of two of the elderly men had begun to fall down, who should present himself in front of me again but the General. He looked at me with disgust and, pointing to my precious red star, the badge of my proficiency, he said, "What's that thing you've got on your arm?"

Something snapped inside me. The words came out before I could stop them. I said crisply, "Star of David, sir. Jewish private." At which, as the saying goes, the shit hit the fan. I was put on report for gross insubordination. My friend Harley was practically in tears.

"With this report against you," he said, "it will be a long time before you will ever become an officer."

So I remained a private for the rest of my time in the Ministry with, I might add, considerable relief.

All the same, I passed the word around to my "general" relatives. One of them said to me, "I know the fellow. He always was a silly bugger. The tropical sun baked all his brains to scrambled eggs. He's junior to me, of course. I might be able to do something about him."

I know my relative went a-hunting for him, but I never learned with what success. He would never have told me anyway; and now they are all commanding their divisions in a Better Place. I hope the liverish old Indian-type is not tugging at the crotch of the Archangel Gabriel.

17

When the war in Europe ended, I left the Ministry of Information and my brief career as a temporary civil servant and joined a firm called Lacrinoid Products Ltd. as sales manager. It was a dull job selling buttons and door furniture, but I mark the events in my life by the friends I have made rather than by the money, and Hans Baum, a German Jew who had fled Germany in 1936 and had come penniless to England, and who was the managing director of Lacrinoid, became one of my closest friends. He was a short, roly-poly man with red hair and an elegant wife, and he deserves special mention.

Much has been written about the eminent scientists,

Jewish and non-Jewish, who fled Germany and who, by lending their immense knowledge to the Allies, helped in Hitler's defeat. Hans was not an eminent scientist, yet you should know about his contribution; for it seems to me to have its own, special place in history.

Just before Hans fled Germany, he had been involved in the experimental molding of men's buttons from urea formaldehyde. Upon arrival in England, he had set up a little factory in a garage in Hampstead, in the north of London. He and his wife made buttons in the morning and in the afternoons went out trying to sell them, and they managed to earn some kind of a living. When the war came, Hans was picked up and, with many other Germans, incarcerated on the Isle of Wight.

There he may well have remained for the duration but for the fact that with Italy's entry into the war, buttons became extremely scarce. Army uniforms had metal buttons, but with the increasing shortage of metals of all kinds, these became scarce, too. It reached the point, in fact, where the British Government regarded the shortage of buttons as a minor national crisis.

The plastics industry was then in its infancy, and when the proposal was made that buttons could be molded, somebody remembered Hans Baum. He was immediately retrieved from the Isle of Wight and made a most useful contribution to the art of molding buttons. The mathematicians, the physicists, and the rocket experts have held the limelight. The fact is, however, that without the contribution of my friend Hans, the British Army might well have had to advance into battle with gaping flies.

Just before joining Lacrinoid I had approached the Ministry of Food about getting a license to import Jamaican rum into England. The import of Jamaican rum into England had been a well-established trade for centuries. But during the war, all imports of bottled rum as opposed to rum in bulk had been prohibited because of the shortage of shipping space.

A friend of mine and a first cousin of Barbara, a man called Eustace Myers, was then the owner of the old family firm of Fred L. Myers and Company, the proprietors of Myers Rum. He had asked me if I could help him to reestablish his exports of bottled rum to Britain by obtaining a license to do so. In this I was fortunately most successful and got the first postwar license granted, which gave Myers a considerable jump on his competitors. For this, he agreed to bottle a special brand of rum for me called Jamaica Club Brand, and I formed a small company to distribute it. This led me to thinking of other products.

One of the things I had noted during the war years was the drinking habits of the lower-middle and working classes of England. The men went into pubs and drank beer, tepid drafts of mild or bitter ale or a mixture of the two, which might as well have been horse-piss so far as I was concerned, though I soon learned that to insult the Englishman's beer was as serious an offense as insulting his King. Their wives or girlfriends, however, did not often drink beer, and, for some reason or another, these classes did not regard the drinking of gin by women as "refined." So while they waited for their men, they drank mostly cherry brandy but not, it seemed to me, with any great relish.

This made me think of a coffee liqueur which my aunt occasionally used to make on one of my uncle's sugar estates. In the old days the wives of estate owners would make small quantities of rum liqueurs for home use. They most often made a delicious liqueur by steeping ripe pimento berries in strong rum which they called Pimento Dram. But they would sometimes make other flavors as well. It occurred to me that a coffee liqueur would be an ideal drink for Englishwomen in pubs. It was not a taste which had to be acquired, and the coffee aspect would make it respectable and "refined." Besides, if the coffee flavor was from genuine coffee beans and not synthetic, such a liqueur would have the stimulating qualities of the caffeine which would neutralize the depressant effect of the alcohol.

There is no such thing in the world as a genuine aphrodisiac (except a new lover) but the nearest approach is a stimulant. If I could lower the inhibitions of the English lower-middle-class woman with alcohol, while giving her a kick in the libido with caffeine, it seemed to me that I'd be making a great contribution to the kind of attention her old man would get when he took her home, an improvement which would be bound to contribute to my financial advantage.

I became immensely enthusiastic, and in 1946 I left Lacrinoid and flew to Jamaica to pay a visit to my aunt in Westmoreland with a view to getting her recipe for a coffee liqueur. When I arrived in Westmoreland my aunt, alas, was in her dotage. She could hardly remember my name, and kept on calling me by the name of a first cousin. Yes, she remembered her coffee liqueur but, no, she couldn't remember how she made it.

I returned to Kingston most discouraged, but a few days afterwards somebody told me that a doctor, a government pathologist by the name of Ken Evans, had for some time had the hobby of making liqueurs of various kinds and that I should go to see him.

My visit to Ken Evans was an enormous success. He had made, experimentally, some excellent rum liqueurs: pimento, orange, lime and, most important of all, coffee. What was more, his scientific mind and precision enabled him to produce the kind of recipe which could be made in bulk without quality variations.

The problem was, however, to get into production. I called in my old friend Herbert Hart, who by this time had returned to Jamaica. One trouble was that I could not get either Ken Evans or Herbert to believe me when I told them that I could sell a first shipment of five thousand cases immediately. They were still thinking of a liqueur as something one sells only in the most expensive hotels, bars and nightclubs. They would not believe me when I told them that our market would be in the pubs and that it would be a vast market.

I bullied them as much as I could; but another problem arose. It was impossible in 1946 to buy the stainless steel vats and other equipment necessary or to get the bottles to put the liqueur in. Herbert solved the equipment problem by bringing in Paul Geddes of Desnoes and Geddes, Jamaica's largest brewery, who had all the equipment we needed, and Eustace Myers solved the bottle problem by giving me a letter of introduction to a top man at Owens-Illinois in New York who had been supplying Myers with bottles for years. As a special favor to Eustace, Owens-Illinois made bottles, caps and cartons available to us.

So, having arranged with Herbert to set up a company called Estate Industries Ltd., I flew back to England leaving Herbert and Ken Evans the job of making our first five thousand cases of coffee liqueur. I was to get the labels designed and have them flown to Jamaica. In the meantime, we had contracted with a Mr. Keeble Munn, who produced the finest Jamaican coffee on his plantation in the Blue Mountains, to supply us with all the coffee we needed. It was a large order, and he was very pleased. No other coffee has ever since been used, as far as I know.

After some time as business manager of the Crown Film Unit at Pinewood, I had been moved up to the Russell Square office of the Ministry of Information to a new section, the head of which was a middle-aged Irishman by the name of Joseph Patrick MacNulty. He had been in the advertising business before the war and, like many other people in advertising, had been put to work at the Ministry doing internal propaganda. I went to Russell Square as J. P. MacNulty's assistant. The kindness of Joe and his wife Helen to my wife and me and to Herbert Hart will never be forgotten by any of us. Joe was a diabetic. Sometime in 1943 he felt that his health could not withstand the strain of his ministry job and he left to return to his small advertising agency, J. P. MacNulty and Company. I took over his job at the ministry when he left.

When I in my turn left the Ministry and got involved in rum and plastics, there was therefore no question as to who should do our advertising. Joe was already involved in the accounts of Lacrinoid, of Myers Rum, and of Jamaica Club Brand. So it was to Joe I went about our new coffee liqueur, including the design of the label. A name for the coffee liqueur had to be found before we could do anything, and Joe and his colleagues racked their brains for days for just the right name without coming up with anything which seemed just right. My brain was, as usual, a blank as it always is when it comes to names for products, for children, or for books.

At a conference one day at Clifford's Inn, where both Joe and I had our offices, we had run through about fifty names, none of which pleased us, so to break the tedium I was telling Joe about trying to get the recipe from my aunt and how I had drawn a blank. Suddenly, Joe leaped to his feet. "I've got it," he shouted. "I know exactly what we'll call that damn liqueur. Aunt Mary–Tia Maria."

And *Tia Maria* it was called.

It was an instant success in English pubs and went on to be a success all over the world. It even gravitated from the pubs into high society and is today one of the largest selling liqueurs in the world.

Herbert Hart and I do not, however, enjoy the great profits which Tia Maria increasingly brings in. We did pretty well out of it, but some years ago we decided to sell the half-share in the project which we jointly owned. It was a bad decision, from the business point of view. We knew this, but we had other and personal reasons for selling. The people who get very rich are usually those who prefer wealth to peace of mind. We chose peace of mind. Even so, it was a paradoxical choice, for the subsequent profits from Tia Maria could have bought a lot of peace of mind.

I nearly wrote at this point that one does not, after all, live in vain. But I have had to revise it. The Minister of Security in the present Jamaican government, who has thrice threatened me with prosecution, is Keeble Munn. I am glad to say, however, that at least the quality of his coffee beans, if not his brains, remains unimpaired.

What with Tia Maria and rum and sundry other activities, I found myself in the immediate postwar period prosperously self-employed. Or rather, I would have been earning a very great deal of money had it not been for the penal British taxation. It was an absurd situation. As each year went along, my accountant would advise me that unless I spent six or seven thousand pounds right away on traveling, which could be charged up to my companies, the British tax collector would get nearly all of it. So my first wife and I would take off for various places for holidays we didn't really want, just to frustrate the Income Tax Commissioner.

Not all the trips were pure holidays, of course. We went once each year to Jamaica via New York and Nassau, mostly on business. All the same, I was pretty damned fed up paying such heavy taxes each year; nearly four times what I was earning for myself even though I had taken some legal tax avoidance procedures. For instance, my friend Eustace Myers had set up a company for me in Nassau which bought Jamaica Club Brand Rum and then sold it to me in England. In this way, we kept some of the profits in tax-free Nassau. But there was a limit to what was legally possible.

During a visit to Jamaica in 1948, I heard that a 720-acre farm, called Charlottenburgh, was up for sale. It was a beautiful place and owned by the DeLisser family. The family had decided at that time to invest heavily in the new hotel industry that was developing in Jamaica, and they needed the extra cash. So I used some of the Nassau profits to buy Charlottenburgh and, as usual, called upon my friend Herbert Hart to help me by looking after the place, as I had to return to England.

I think I would have lived in England permanently after the war had it not been for the Commissioner of Income Tax. My first wife and I were happily settled in a delightful flat in Kensington and, after seven years in London, we had made a lot of friends. But one morning in 1948, before going to Jamaica that year, I had had a session with my accountant. I realized that all the fourteen-hour days I had been putting in since the end of 1944 had mostly been for the benefit of the tax commissioner. It was obviously a mugg's game. I decided that I was no longer going to be a party to this treadmill, a victim of a kind of national Mafia which heisted three-quarters of one's earnings in what amounted to a legal protection racket. For three centuries the English had exploited my country to build up their own financial institutions, and I came to the conclusion that I would be damned before I worked like a modern-day slave to help them buy their free false teeth.

I figured the English had had years of good fortune: the Scots had built their bridges for them; the Irish had written their best books and plays; the Welsh had dug their coal, and the Colonies had supplied them with raw materials at knock-down prices.

The English had been marvelous during the war. Their courage and calmness had, I believed, saved the world. But it was quite obvious that the British working classes had decided that from 1945 onwards the world owed them a living, and they intended to do as little work as possible.

So I decided when I bought Charlottenburgh that it was to be my thirty-fifth birthday present to myself, and that I would return home in 1949, wrap up my three companies and put them on the shelf, and never do a thing again in my life except farm.

18

My wife and I returned to Jamaica at the end of 1949 and early in 1950 we took up residence in Charlottenburgh.

The farm had run down badly during the war; it had virtually no crops on it and most of it had gone back to bush. I don't think nonfarmers understand how much capital is required to set up a modern farm. Certainly, I had underestimated it. The place needed the immediate planting of two hundred acres of bananas; the cane fields needed extension; cattle had to be bought; fences needed repair. What was worse was that the so-called cottages in which many of the farm workers lived were not, in my view, fit for pigs. They were dirty, unpainted hovels in which some families lived four or five to one ten-by-ten room. They would all have to be pulled down and rebuilt.

First things had to come first. I calculated that the priority would have to be the planting of the bananas so that the farm could be put into a condition to make a profit. Then I could plow back all the profits into making the farm a fit place for people to live and work. It was important to get the new planting done fast. By the middle of the following year, 1951, as a result of enormous expenditure and effort, the new planting was well underway. My first wife had worked miracles with the three acres around the house, and we had the beginnings of a beautiful garden.

Then came the hurricane of 1951. Most West Indian hurricanes form in the southeastern Caribbean or in the South Atlantic and spiral their way west and north, gathering strength as they go. Sometimes they blow themselves out over the sea. Sometimes they miss all land masses and disappear in the Atlantic north of Cuba. Sometimes they hit Jamaica or Cuba or Florida or Central America around the Gulf of Mexico. It is difficult to predict their courses for they change them as they travel along. Their forward speed is slow, usually at about ten miles an hour, but the speed of the wind within the whirling mass of air can be up to one hundred and fifty miles an hour.

Insofar as it is possible to speak of the usual course of West Indian hurricanes, Jamaica is not within that course. Jamaica regularly suffers near misses which bring torrential rains and very high winds, but on the average—every thirty years or so—Jamaica does get a direct hit and all hell breaks loose.

We had all been watching the course of this hurricane for some days. It had been trundling along at about five miles an hour, directly towards us. Its slow forward speed meant that it was a very large hurricane, for the larger the air mass, the slower it travels. As usual, the hurricane was being tracked by U. S. aircraft, and its position reported three or four times a day.

By the afternoon of the night it hit us, I knew we were in for trouble. The air at Charlottenburgh was still and warm and the clouds were piling up mountainously high upon the horizon. The hurricane warnings were out, and the red flags were flying from the roofs of the post offices. By six o'clock I had the house all battened down. Wooden shutters, made for the purpose, were nailed over all the glass windows. Jalousies were nailed shut. The garage doors and the front and back doors were barred and nailed with four-inch nails. All animals were taken indoors.

At that time, we had no public electricity supply at Charlottenburgh though we had the telephone, so the lamps were brought into the house and prepared in the usual way. By seven in the evening, the heavy rains had started.

I felt we would be pretty safe in the house. The house had been newly built for me in 1949. I had seen to it that the roof was supported on reinforced concrete pillars to which it was anchored by thick, ten-inch steel bolts. It was a low, bungalow-type of house which didn't offer much resistance to wind. And I knew that so long as a window or door didn't blow in, nothing much would happen. The trick with hurricanes is to keep the doors and windows intact. Once a door blows in the wind gets in and lifts the roof off.

It had happened with Strawberry Hill, our mountain house in St. Andrew, when I was five years old. The front door blew in and, to this day, I remember huddling against Nanny and my mother and watching in astonishment as the whole roof slowly lifted more or less in one piece and disappeared. When the hurricane was over, my father found the roof neatly deposited in a valley a mile away and a thousand feet below. We had all escaped without injury, every one of us including the cat, because a large built-in cupboard provided shelter. We had emerged having suffered nothing more serious than a monstrous fright and a prolonged soaking.

The cat, I think, had been more indignant than anyone else, and my father the most covered in mud. He had been in Kingston, as usual, and when the hurricane warning had been issued—for in those days there was no radio and warnings came at the last moment—he had leaped into his Model T Ford to drive furiously up into the mountains to be with us.

Model T Fords had certain eccentricities. One of them was that if you were going to drive up a steep hill, you had to see that the gas tank was full. This was because the gas tank was in front of the driver, under the hood, and the gas feed was by gravity. If the tank was fairly empty and you were pointed up a steep hill, the gas couldn't flow to the carburetor.

In my father's haste and anxiety to reach Strawberry Hill from our house in Kingston, he forgot to check the gas—with the consequence that when he was within a mile of us on the steepest part of the road, the Ford refused to go another step. My father, like other Ford Model T owners, knew the answer, which was to turn the car around and go up the hill backwards. The gas would then flow happily once again. The trouble was that the hurricane was by then upon him, and he couldn't see to drive backwards because of the blinding rain. He abandoned the Ford and traveled the remaining mile on his belly. In a hurricane it's not possible to stand upright against the wind, and exceedingly dangerous even if you could, for everything comes adrift, the boughs of trees, sheets of corrugated iron and bits of woods act like missiles. He reached us in a torrent of water and mud and evil language. Still, his presence cheered us up enormously.

On that night in 1951 at Charlottenburgh, the wind began in earnest at about nine p.m. and howled like a thousand banshees the whole night through. All our doors and windows held, but the rain, blown by winds in excess of one hundred miles an hour, came under the doors and through every crack and crevice in the windows, and the floors were soaked. With every gust of wind, the walls shook.

By morning, the hurricane had more or less blown itself out, and at eight o'clock I thought it safe to go outside and take a look. Barbara came with me, and we unashamedly wept at what we saw. Her garden was in ruins. The driveway to the house was blocked by a tangle of fallen trees, telephone poles and lines, assorted bits of trees, and old corrugated iron sheets. It took me an hour with the help of my staff, wielding cutlasses and axes, to chop a way for my jeep to pass. When I was eventually able to get about to see the damage, I found that my overseer's house—which had been the old Great House—had been seriously damaged. The verandahs on all sides had been blown to pieces, and the roof was leaking.

Every banana tree I had planted, as well as a good many other trees, were flat on the ground. The roads were blocked by fallen trees or eroded by the heavy rain. Fifteen inches of rain had fallen in eight hours, and one curious result fascinated me—even in my general misery. I had planted some young citrus trees. In one spot in one field, in an area in which six trees had been planted twenty feet apart, the deep clay had become fluid with the rain and must have flowed slowly like very thick treacle. The six trees were standing, wind-harrassed but otherwise upright, relatively undamaged, but they were all a good fifteen feet from where they had been planted. The earth had simply moved them, roots and all, to a new location.

All my work and money was down the drain. I would have to start all over again.

The hurricane of 1951 had hit the south and east of Jamaica with full force. St. Mary, the parish in which Charlottenburgh is located, was cut off from Kingston for four days. All telephone lines were down. All roads were impassable.

The Inspector of Police for the parish had been unable to make other than radio contact with Kingston. On the second day after the hurricane, hearing I was anxious to find out how my parents had fared in their house in Kingston, he said that he would assign me a motorcycle escort if I would attempt to get through to Kingston somehow and deliver some messasges for him. I had, at that time, a five-ton Fargo truck. I put six of my men on it, with axes and cutlasses, and started off for Kingston by a roundabout route, accompanied by a policeman on a motorcycle who was supposed to ride ahead. I drove the truck myself.

I soon had to load the policeman and his cycle onto the truck. The whole route to Kingston looked as if the island had been hit by an atomic bomb. We chopped our way through, manhandling the truck through rivers and through mud. It took us six hours to make a journey of thirty-five miles. Kingston had had a bad time. My parents' house had suffered ten thousand pounds' worth of damage. All power was off. My parents had not, however, suffered any physical injury.

These "acts of God" always are worse in the more developed places. At Charlottenburgh, for instance, as we had no electricity anyway, we did not miss the lack of it. We had the kind of refrigerator that worked, paradoxically, by a flame fed by kerosene oil. In Kingston, my parents, like everyone else, were without light and power. In consequence, all the food in their refrigerator and deep freeze had gone bad.

Just before I set off for Kingston, I had packed two of my lamps (the kind of lamps that work with a gas mantle and compressed kerosene oil), a lot of ice cubes which I had wrapped in masses of old newspaper, and two chickens my wife had cooked. When I arrived at my parents' home with these gifts, you would have thought I had brought them a King's ransom—even though six hours on the road had not done anything very much for the ice cubes.

It took me two years and every penny I had, plus more

that I had to borrow, to put Charlottenburgh back on its feet. Sometimes I didn't know how I was going to find the money for the payroll at the end of the week, and I had some very close shaves. One good thing was that the hurricane had wrecked most of the pigsties which went under the name of worker's cottages. I built twenty nice new ones, installing running water and electricity (when electricity finally came to us) in most of them. We ran a competition each year for the most pleasant little garden around each.

The effect upon the workers who lived in them was dramatic. All of a sudden they were dressing better; they were keeping their children neat and tidy, and sending them to school; they were holding their heads up.

At the same time, I had instituted free medical services for all my employees, who numbered about eighty. This must be slightly qualified. Jamaica had had quite a good and, more or less free, medical service for years–long before England had one. But as it meant going to government hospitals and queueing up, most of the peasantry did not find it convenient for ordinary, routine medical attention. What I did was to arrange with a local doctor to give my workers such routine or emergency attention as they needed. If they needed surgery, we would arrange for them to be admitted without delay into the local hospital where they would get attention at public expense in the usual way.

I then tried a new experiment with some unexpected results. All farm work in Jamaica is done by piece rates. Woe to anyone who thinks he can get any work done by a weekly paid employee, except in very special circumstances. So the rate for each job is fixed by the union or by agreement with the workers. It is often a very tedious business. Apart from this, one of the interesting though puzzling things about Jamaica is the way the soil varies, even within a small area. One field may be excellent for growing bananas while the field right next to it will only grow citrus. In theory, this can be sorted out by having soil analyses made by the government's agricultural chemist.

I soon found out at great personal expense that in practice the agricultural chemists were nearly always wrong. Indeed, I discovered early that any farmer who allowed himself to be guided by the Jamaican government's agricultural specialists and advisors would be choosing the quickest possible route to bankruptcy. There was a much better way. The workers on Charlottenburgh, whether they lived in one of my cottages or not (for many had their own small farms nearby), had mostly been working on the place all their lives. The older ones especially knew from memory and experience exactly what kind of soil was best for what kind of crop. I had all the expertise I needed.

So, with all my fellow-farmers telling me that I was stark staring mad, I set up a small committee of my workers—which I called the "managing committee." This committee was actually elected by the workers, except for my headman who sat on it as of right. I did not. I only came in a consultative capacity, and I had no vote, though I was careful to reserve for myself the power of veto just in case.

The job of this committee was twofold. It was first to fix all rates for all jobs. Secondly, it was to decide what was going to be planted where and when and the nature of the maintenance needed.

From the very beginning, the committee worked like a charm. It had access to all my accounts, though in practice I had to do a lot of explaining and interpreting because most of the committee members couldn't read, let alone read a balance sheet. This committe ran my farm.

The most surprising result arose in the matter of rates, and it was only concerning this that I ever had to use my veto power. While they fixed rates which were somewhat higher than the union rates—which I would have done anyway—they were never unreasonably high. The trouble came once the rates had been fixed because, at this point, the honor of the committee was at stake. Thus, if any worker started to raise a fuss about the rates, this would be taken by the committee as a personal affront.

On one occasion, the committee had fixed rates for a job which was out of the ordinary, and some of the men involved had complained and a big fuss had started. The members of the committee took a most diehard view. The complainers, they told me, either had to be fired or they would feel the sharp edge of the committee members' cutlasses. This seemed to me to be carrying things a bit far, and I had to use my veto. I was not popular for weeks.

The situation at Charlottenburgh also had another peculiar result. I had done everything during my first five years to give my workers a sense of self-respect: to make them feel that I loved them—which was, in any event, the simple truth. I used to pile them into my truck and take them swimming at a small beach I had acquired, and we would have curried goat feasts every so often and drink a lot of rum. One day the local inspector of police came to me and said rather severely that it was time that I controlled my men better.

"You have about forty extremely tough gentlemen who are getting out of hand," he said.

This surprised me for I had found them very easy to deal with.

"In what way?" I asked.

"Don't you know?" he said. "They have a habit of going to Richmond on Friday nights and wrecking the place."

"No, I don't know," I said with complete truthfulness.

"They are an arrogant bunch. They get drunk and raise hell and, then, when the policeman speaks to them, they say he dare not put them in jail because of you."

"I have never said anything like that."

"I know you haven't. But you go and bail them—don't

you? And defend them when they come up for trial. And get them off because you confuse the prosecution. It's not good enough."

I had, indeed, defended two or three with success, but I had no idea the matter had gone this far.

"It's not for me to say what you are to do," the inspector continued, "but I would greatly appreciate it if you would help to control your people. They think they are too special."

So I called everyone together after payday one Friday and told them that they had to behave better. They denied everything. According to them, all their visits to Richmond were like Sunday School outings.

On the following Sunday morning my headman came to the house. Five of my men were in jail. Could I go and "spring" them as usual?

They were in jail for various charges ranging from drunkenness to Assault Occasioning Bodily Harm.

It was too damn much. I let them stay in the lockup for two days until they came before the magistrate. Then I defended them and got them off. Privately, I compensated the two policemen whom they had bashed, and each week deducted from the pay of the five men the compensation I had paid the policemen. That fixed it. Richmond thereafter rested in relative peace on Friday nights. In Jamaica, if you are wise, you go about things in a very roundabout way.

19

The dream of retiring from an active life of business at thirty-five and spending the rest of my days farming in Paradise had to be, I suppose, as insubstantial as any other dream.

Bobby Alexander, an old friend who had beaten me in a boxing match at the Ward Theatre in Kingston many years ago, started the rot. He wanted to advertise his large real estate business on the radio and had the idea that what he wanted was a soft-sell in dignified circumstances. He wanted me to write and broadcast a series of ten-minutes essays—"amusing, but informative," he said, on any subject I liked—which he would sponsor.

I am sure that from the point of view of selling real estate, he wasted his money, but I had great fun doing the series and, if that is any compensation to him, I was secretly grateful to him for stirring me out of my bucolic torpor. Perhaps that was what the sneaky son of a bitch had in mind in the first place and, if so, he chalked up yet another win on points. One thing led to another, and before I knew it I was in all kinds of radio work, from delivering morning commentaries to writing half-hour radio plays.

In the meantime, another old friend, Theodore Sealy, at that time the very distinguished editor of the Jamaican *Daily Gleaner*, asked me in 1952 if I thought I could write a column. I told him I hadn't the faintest idea how to do it but that I would try. I began with one column a week of about twelve hundred words. I was soon doing two a week. Then three. Then, ultimately, five columns a week. The column, for some reason or another, was an almost immediate success, and even modesty, real or false, will not deter me from saying that I have become the widest-read columnist in the history of the West Indian press. My radio commentary also became a record-breaker.

At thirty-seven, I had begun a whole new career.

I think the basic reason why my column has been so successful and my radio broadcasts so well received, is really very simple. In the West Indies and especially in Jamaica, there was a very wide gap between how people spoke and how they wrote. Writing in colonial outposts had to be very circumspect. You couldn't, for example, be flippant about the governor any more than you could be flippant about God. If you did write upon any serious subject, you had to write very seriously and earnestly—due respect had to be paid all around, and so on, and so forth.

I was born with an incapacity to take any of our more solemn institutions very seriously. I am no anarchist. I believe in having institutions. I take the same view of institutions as I take of an earnest belief in the fires of Hell. They are essential to public order. I think it is terribly important for people to believe in them. I would not alter the whole solemn procession of kings, president, archbishops, lawlords, bankers, generals, corporate chairmen, and so on, right down to the Elks, the Rotarians and the Kiwanis, even if I could. I can't take them very seriously—that's all—any more than I can take seriously the assorted revolutionaries and idealists who would seek to replace our existing institutions with their own new editions of kings, presidents, archbishops, etc.

It has been said a thousand times that the only creative endeavor over which any of us have full control is the living of our own lives. Like any other work of art, a frame is needed and our institutions are the frames within which we must paint our own pictures. Michelangelo would have painted just as superbly had his sponsor been Consolidated Edison rather than the Church of Rome.

It is important only to have a multiplicity of institutions within whose limitations there is scope for individual expression. There is only one evil as great as the monolithic state as the sole institution. That would be no institutions at all. In the first case the individual cannot creatively operate, and in the second both art and life would become meaningless without disciplines and restraints.

So, in writing my column and my broadcasts. I have never been encumbered with a deep belief in current myths and institutions and so could put a distance between them and what I wrote. I wrote as I spoke, not as local tradition said I must write; and whatever I wanted to say, I said.

This came, at first, as a great shock to people—not because I was writing anything really shocking, but because I was just being myself. Without the support of Theodore Sealy, I think I would have been prevented from continuing, but Theo stood by me and encouraged me. Finally people began to feel that I was writing what they had really felt all the time but had not wanted to admit even to themselves. Of course, not everyone liked this kind of exercise. The pompous hated it. This was splendid grist to my mill.

So, by 1958, I was not only farming, but was six years into my new career, working very hard and having a marvelous time.

At which point disaster, one might say, struck.

There was an elderly man in St. Mary by the name of H. S. Schliefer. He was a descendant of one of the many German craftsmen who had come to Jamaica in the early nineteenth century. He had become a wealthy landowner and had spent a life in good works and local politics. He was a pillar of the Church and of the Jamaica Labour Party.

Schliefer was as fond of me as I was of him, and he was forever trying to get me, as a landowner, into lending a hand with local politics, an effort which I was resisting strongly. But there was a point with old H. S. at which resistance became unwise. He is a rather imperious old man and brooked no nonsense from anyone. One day, for example, he discovered a secret I had been hiding from him—which was that on my father's side I am descended from Donald Cargill, the covenanter known as the Rattray Martyr. As old H. S. was an enthusiastic Presbyterian, he was outraged not only that I did not attend church, but that I did not attend *his* church.

In order to get me into a situation I could not easily resist, I was invited to attend the reopening of the local Presbyterian church which had been closed to have electricity installed. I was asked to turn on the first light.

After the service of dedication, I was ushered between two parsons to an electric light bulb hanging from the ceiling, and the packed congregation was told that I would turn it on after the hymn, which was "Lead Kindly Light." By this time, I was wondering what to say and suffering slightly from the jitters. So, when my turn came, I grasped the switch and said, with remarkable lack of originality, but in a firm voice: "Let there be light!" and pushed the switch.

Nothing whatever happened. No lights came on. There was a blank moment of hushed silence. Then from the back of the church old H. S. Schliefer's powerful voice boomed out, "Don't you hear? Let there be light!"

And on the lights came. Old H. S. wouldn't stand any nonsense, even from the Almighty. I was careful not to offend him.

One morning in early 1958 he telephoned me.

"Morris," he said in his usual imperious way, "you are going to help me with something this afternoon. The local branch of the Jamaican Labour Party is having a big meeting at the schoolhouse in Richmond to elect a candidate for St. Mary for the federal elections. I want you to come onto the platform and propose L. E. A. Francis. He's a good man, and I want him as our candidate. Now don't fail me. Come at four." And he hung up, not bothering to wait for an answer.

It seemed a harmless enough thing to ask me. I had always supported Sir Alexander Bustamante and his Labour Party, and L. E. A. Francis, our local druggist, was a delightful and intelligent man. I could think of no better candidate. I would propose him with pleasure.

So on I went to the meeting at four-thirty, allowing, as always, a half-hour difference between Jamaican time and Greenwich Mean Time. I found the schoolroom packed with about four hundred Jamaica Labour Party delegates and supporters. The meeting had just started, and I was invited onto the platform. Another old friend, a local lawyer called Sydney Phillips, was acting as chairman. Old H. S. and about five other leading citizens made up the rest of the group on the platform.

Sydney Phillips explained the purpose of the meeting and

then called for nominations for federal candidates, which nominations would have to be moved and seconded from the Floor. Two of the men on the platform nominated two different candidates. In neither case could a Mover or a Seconder be found for them. No particular reaction seemed to be coming from the Floor at all. The delegates were strangely silent.

"Your turn now," said old H. S. to me in a hoarse whisper.

I got up. "Mr. Chairman," I said, "I beg to nominate our much-respected Mr. L. E. A. Francis, known to all as Doc Francis."

I didn't exactly expect a standing ovation, but I was shocked when my proposal was met with stony silence.

"Any Mover or Seconder?" asked the Chairman.

Absolute silence.

"In which case," said Sydney Phillips in what was now obvious desperation, "there being no further nominations from the platform, the meeting is now thrown open to nominations from the Floor."

"What is wrong with them all?" said old H. S. in a loud voice.

A short, fat man stood up. "Mr. Chairman, sir," he said. "We listened to the proposals from the platform with respect. They is all good men. But we here on de Floor only want one man. He don't know it yet, but he goin' to know it now. I beg to nominate"—and here he paused for effect—"I beg to nominate Mr. Morris Cargill."

At which point all hell broke lose in a meeting which until a few seconds ago was the quietest I had ever attended. Everyone started to stamp and shout. I thought for one horrifying moment they were shouting down the proposal and were about to boo me. Then it hit me. They all began to chant my name in unison.

I turned to Sydney and said, "This is utterly preposterous! Who the hell put them up to it?"

"Nobody." said Sidney. "I swear to you. At least nobody from the platform."

"Do you know anything about this?" I asked H. S.

"I give you my word, Morris; I know nothing. But now you must stand."

"I will do nothing of the sort." I said.

The noise was now deafening. Sydney asked for silence and eventually got it. Then he said, "Gentlemen, this nomination comes as a surprise to all of us. We are adjourning for a few minutes in order to confer with Mr. Cargill outside."

I went out to the back of the building with all the others on the platform. They turned to me one by one.

"We've never seen anything like this." said one. "You cannot let them down. You must stand!"

"But—Jesus Christ! I don't know anything about getting elected!" I protested.

"Do not call the Lord's name in vain." said old H. S. "You must stand."

Everybody was now talking at once. Eventually I said, "Right. I'll do it if you let me speak to the delegates first."

So back we went, to be greeted with a roar and more shouts of "Cargill! Cargill!" So I got up and called for silence. I told them that I was the wrong candidate. I was white. I was the descendant of slaveowners. I was totally inexperienced. I didn't know how to run an election. I didn't, I added, even think much of the Federal idea. But, I added, if they still wanted me, I'd do it.

If there had been an uproar before, there was now complete confusion. The people on the floor rushed the platform. They picked me up, shouting "Until they elect you, your feet will never again touch the ground!" They carried me—or rather manhandled me—to my car, into which they unceremoniously dumped me. When at last I managed to get home, my jacket half off, my tie askew, my collar open and my shirt torn, Barbara thought that I had been in a fight and nearly fainted. And she nearly fainted again when she learned that I was now the new JLP candidate for the federal election. Now that I had time to think, the whole thing appalled me.

I drove immediately to my farm, for it was still light. There were about twenty people standing about. I told them what had happened. They listened carefully. Then one of them said, "Don't worry, Bossy. We will go out on our bicycles on weekends. We will run the election for you. The people will carry you in. You will see."

Another said with a laugh, "We knew all this already, you know, Bossy. There was much talk of it for de last week. You not telling us any news."

I said, "Well, for God's sake, couldn't you have told me?"

The man replied, "It is not good sometimes for you to know certain things, Bossy."

They all nodded and laughed again as another said, "Not all the time for you to know too much."

As I have said: In Jamaica, if you are wise, you go about things in a very roundabout way.

I went home to the strongest vodka and tonic I could find and felt a lot better. If I was going to fight an election, well, I was going to fight it as best I could.

General elections in Jamaica can sometimes be a bit rough, with rocks and bottles being thrown about and a few heads getting split. In this respect, the federal elections in St. Mary got off to a bad start.

On Nomination Day, which begins the official process of an election, both candidates have to go to be nominated; so Ivan Cameron, my opponent, and I had to go to the Courthouse at Anmotto Bay. As usual, the square outside the courthouse was crowded with supporters of both sides, and political feelings were running high. Nevertheless, everything went off relatively peacefully during nomination.

Barbara had driven me to Anmotto Bay, about ten miles from where we lived, and one of my workers, a man called

Campbell, had come with us. After the short nomination ceremony, I walked back to my car through the crowd without incident, with Campbell by my side. As we reached the car, Campbell got in first (it was a two-door model) to sit in the back, and I got into the front next to Barbara.

Just as we were about to move off, a man rushed up to the side of the car on which my wife sat. He had a mouth organ gripped in his fist and he swung his fist through the open window, missing Barbara's head by a fraction of an inch, as he aimed at Campbell in the rear seat. The sharp edge of the mouth organ caught Campbell a glancing blow on the scalp, cutting his scalp badly and causing the blood to jet all over my wife.

Campbell yelled, "Stop!" In a few seconds, he and I were out of the car in hot pursuit of the man, who had turned and fled. In a few seconds more, Campbell had caught up with the man. He hit the man with a left and then a right, and laid him out as if he were laying a carpet. We then returned to the car, and my wife drove off, with Campbell's scalp wound, as scalp wounds do, covering the seat of the car with blood, as if we had been butchering a pig. He had four stitches put in as soon as we could get him to a doctor.

I knew my opponent, Ivan Cameron, quite well. He was a banana selector and had a very small farm of his own. He was a delightful man, and I liked him. So I went to see him, which in Jamaican elections is very much frowned upon, especially after Nomination Day. We agreed that we would do everything we could to keep our supporters away from violence. On the whole, we succeeded.

I equipped myself rather well for the election, and my friend Sydney Phillips went out of his way to raise a good deal of money for my expenses. I fitted up my five-ton truck as a moving election platform. Electioneering in a parish like St. Mary involved going out night after night into countless little areas tucked away in the bush and in the hills, and into small villages and small towns. Few of these places had any electric light, and the traditional method was to do one's electioneering from behind a small table with a lantern on it, set outside a shop, with the audience more or less in total darkness.

I altered all that. My truck had two large batteries and a portable electric generator, which was carefully muffled, and it was fitted up with spotlights to illuminate the entire area, and a string of lights over the platform set up in the body of the truck. It also had four loud-speakers connected to microphones and a record player, which provided music and enough volume for the speakers to waken the dead.

Barbara, whose hobby was painting, had painted for me a most excellent, large map of the entire Caribbean on a huge window blind. This was set up behind the platform on the truck. All I had to do was to pull down the blind and there I was, equipped to give a lecture on the islands which were to be federated. I also recruited a few girls to sing party songs over the microphones. All we had to do was to go into any area—no matter how isolated—and open our circus. The electric lights alone attracted people to the meeting.

It was an exhausting campaign, however, and because I had to go out night after night, I got very short of sleep. I had to stop writing and broadcasting because I now no longer could be considered an impartial commentator. During the election, too, I had my first and last strike on Charlottenburgh.

It was a very odd strike. One day my farm manager came to me to say that all my workers were on strike. They had gathered in a very large shed we had and were demanding to see me. He advised that I come right away.

I found the whole thing puzzling. My workers had consistently refused, ever since I had taken over Charlottenburgh, to join a trade union, and we had never had an angry word about rates of pay, thanks to the managing committee. Indeed, their refusal to join the trade union had become a bit of an embarrassment when I had gone into politics. In Jamaica, the two major political parties are founded upon their trade unions: the BITU for the Labour Party, and the NWU for the People's National Party.

The fact that I was standing as the Labour Party's candidate seemed to demand that my employees should at least join the BITU. I spoke to them about it, but with some misgiving, for they were all using their spare time to help me to fight my election, and I did not want to burden them with further problems.

Eventually, the managing committee came to me to say that while they regarded all union organizers as a bunch of scoundrels, the workers had agreed to join the BITU for a few months. Now, according to the farm manager, they were on strike.

When I got down to the shed about seventy of my workers were collected there, and they greeted me—to my surprise—with a round of applause. An elderly man who was clearly their spokesman for the occasion pulled up a chair and asked me to sit down. So I sat down and asked them what all the trouble was about

"It is like this, Bossy," said the spokesman. "We have three traitors in our midst. And, until you run them off the property, not a fork is touching dutty [ground]. Not a cutlass chopping a banana."

"How do you mean *traitors*?" I asked.

"They are traitors because they are PNP comrades."

"But, look," I said, "they are doing their work well. I cannot fire people because they don't agree with my politics."

I then launched into a pompous lecture, I fear, on the meaning of parliamentary democracy and freedom of speech. They listened to me carefully and politely. When I was finished, the spokesman said, "We hear you, Bossy, but you are a young man in politics. You do not understand how it goes. You must be advised by we who are older. We will not work with traitors."

"Well," I said, getting a little angry, "I will not fire them, and that is that. If that is the recommendation of the managing committee, I veto it!"

There was a silence. It was a silence which seemed to last a very long time as we sat glaring at one another. Then the spokesman said, "It seems that the time has come for compromise."

"Yes, indeed it has," I replied.

"We will look after the compromise and send to let you know. You go back to your house, Bossy, and take it easy. We will find a solution."

So, not knowing what else to say or do, I left and went back to the house. An hour later, my farm manager came up grinning from ear to ear. 'The people are back to work," he told me.

"Good. I'm glad they took to heart what I told them."

"Well, I don't rightly know if that is the case," he replied.

"What do you mean?"

"Well, Bossy, to tell the truth, I don't really know. All I know is that I see the three comrades running down the road. And the rest of the men after them. I think the comrades have compromised by deciding not to come back." And he said it with a dead straight face. They had dealt me a stacked hand from the start.

Eventually, the Federal Election campaign drew to its close. I had gone by truck, jeep, muleback, and on foot, to every corner of the Parish of St. Mary. I had made more than one hundred and fifty speeches—or rather, I had made more or less the same speech one hundred and fifty times and had practically bored myself to death. I had a wonderful team of organizers, and the people on my farm took turns in coming with me to meetings during the week and then going out on weekends on house-to-house canvassing. I began by knowing nothing about running an election campaign, but ended up being quite an expert.

On election night we all stayed at home to listen to the results come in on the radio. About forty of my workers came up to the house, and we all sat around on the floor consuming large quantities of rum. As the results began to come in for St. Mary, my opponent jumped off with a big leap and halfway through was about fifteen hundred votes ahead. Three of my most enthusiastic workers went outside and threw up, not so much from the rum, but mostly from tension and distress. Four were in tears. Then suddenly the tide turned, and my votes began to flow in. Shortly, I knew I had to win, but even so at the end of the count the size of my majority surprised me. I had come home at a canter.

We consumed two cases of rum that night. The next morning I had such an appalling hangover that I never thought I would live to go to Trinidad.

Just before I left for Trinidad Noël Coward came for dinner. He had heard that Princess Margaret was to be in Trinidad to open Parliament. Noël had known the Princess since her childhood and said to me, "Morris, if you happen to meet Margaret in Trinidad, please tell her I am well and send my love."

Shortly after the arrival of the new MPs and Senators in Port of Spain, we were all summoned to the Governor-General's resident to meet Princess Margaret officially. The new Governor-General was Lord Hailes. He had a most elegant wife, and dressed up in all their scrambled eggs they made an uncommonly handsome pair. All the MPs were put to stand in a straight line, the idea being that the Princess would walk down the line shaking hands and making a brief, polite remark to each of us. The thing that stood out a mile was that with one exception, I was the only white man in the whole line.

When the Princess got to me, I felt that this would probably be the only chance I would have to deliver Noël's message. So I said, "Ma'am, Noël Coward has asked me to tell you he is in Jamaica and well. And he sends his love to you."

Her face lit up with pleasure, and she began to ask a number of questions about Noël, of whom she was clearly fond. So there she stuck in the line chatting before she moved on for the rest of her brief encounters.

When the ceremony was over, all the reporters swarmed around me asking why the Princess had paused so long and what we had spoken about. I had no intention of exposing a personal message and refused to answer. This did not satisfy the reporters, and they all started to shout at me at once. It is in such circumstances that I have never learned to keep my mouth shut. I snapped, "You want to know? Well, then, she said to me, 'Dr. Livingston, I presume?' " It was, to say the least of it, a most unfortunate remark. I was in a good deal of hot water for a week.

Lord and Lady Hailes were, as I said, a most handsome couple, and I cannot think of any other couple I know who so marvelously looked the part they had to play. The only trouble was that Lord Hailes was a bird-brain. His attention span was about ten seconds. I don't think he ever, for a moment, grasped the essentials of the job he had been sent out from England to do. Moreover, he confused being democratic with being undignified. Carried away by Calypsoland, he contrived to fill the beautiful residence with people in hot shirts, and one evening as the head footman was at the top of the stairs announcing the guests, I was astonished to hear him announce in his formal stentorian voice: "My Lord and Lady Fly."

On one occasion, Barbara and I went to a formal lunch at which their were two senators and their wives—all Hindus. To my astonishment, the main course was roast beef. The senator's wife on my left turned to me in some confusion and whispered, "What do I do? Do I refuse it or just play around with it?"

The Hindu senators looked at one another, and one of them said to Lord Hailes, "I hope you don't mind if I pass this course, but I am on a strict diet." Even then the penny refused to drop.

After lunch I thought I really ought to mention the matter to Hailes so, when I got an opportunity to be alone with him, I said, "You shouldn't have served roast beef to Hindus, you know."

"Oh, yes," he said, "sacred cows and all that. My bloody *aide de camp* should have known better." And, with that, his ten-second attention span having been exceeded, he went on to other matters. I do not know whether he ever apologized to the senators. I am sure he must have. Englishmen usually have marvelously good manners—even when they have heads of ivory.

I became, eventually, deputy leader of the Opposition in the Federal House. The proceedings in the Federal Parliament soon became quite pointless. I had a file marked. "Top Secret," in which I used to conceal various books which I read during our endless debates over nothing.

I managed to catch up upon a lot of reading. I read again the whole of Gibbons's *Decline and Fall of the Roman Empire*, and about a dozen of Agatha Christie's detective stories, to name a few. Then I resigned from the Federal House and went home and reported to Sir Alexander Bustamante, the leader of my party, that I thought the whole federal effort was a big nonsense and harmful to Jamaica—to find that he had already firmly come to that conclusion.

In the end, consequent upon the pressures exerted by the Labour Party and by public opinion, Norman Manley—who was then Prime Minister and who was in favor of federation —did a most honorable and statesmanlike thing. Without being required to do so by any Constitutional enactment, he put his belief in federation upon the block and called a referendum—a move bitterly opposed by his son, Jamaica's present Prime Minister.

Norman Manley and those in favor of federation lost the referendum. A general election was called, which Norman Manley and his party also lost. The Jamaica Labour Party returned to power in Jamaica, and the Federation of the West Indies was at an end.

I was supposed to continue in politics, but I told Sir Alexander that politics was not for me. I enjoyed fighting an election, but winning condemned me to a pattern of life that I hated. So I returned to my beloved Charlottenburgh and to writing and broadcasting.

Perhaps I was wrong, but one really has to have a great urge for power to be a successful politician in the latter part of the twentieth century. One has to lose one's amateur status, which is why, of course, our modern politicians make such an immense mess of the world we live in. The compulsion to success guarantees that they must. The paradox is beyond me. The truly honest *successful* politician, and I use the term "honest" to encompass intellectual as well as financial honesty, is as much a logical contradiction as a virginal whore.

20

Barbara and I were divorced in 1973 after thirty-five years of marriage and almost a lifetime of shared experience, for we had known one another from childhood. It might be thought that if a couple could remain married to each other for that length of time, they might as well stick together for the rest of the way. I will always regret that this did not happen. A marriage that long is a kind of joint construction, and its breakup is like the burning down of a house which has been carefully and lovingly built, brick by brick, and furnished with the utmost care.

One of these days I shall try to write a book about my

first marriage, if only to try to explain to myself why I could not any longer sustain a marriage to a woman for whom I have high regard and great affection and who had given me more loyalty than I deserved. Perhaps these things are simpler than we like to make them. A friend, hearing about our divorce, explained: "Oh, Morris is just being a shit."

But if only for my own self-respect I like to think that that is an oversimplification.

Perhaps some marriages, like even the best machinery, just wear out after a time. We tend to forget that when monogamous marriage was postulated many thousands of years ago, the average life expectancy was about forty-six and was still not a great deal higher even as recently as the nineteenth century. A couple, married at twenty-five until death did them part, could not on the average look forward to more than twenty-five years of marriage, if that. Fifty, forty, or even thirty years of marriage was until quite recently wildly unlikely.

My doctor-brother tells me that current longevity and, what is more, longevity in reasonably good health, has created a host of new medical problems such as, for example, maintaining women in good shape for many years past their menopause—a problem which was not very acute when so many women, exhausted by childbearing, were old at fifty and dead by sixty. But now, especially in America, they expect to live to a ripe seventy-five at least, enjoying the money and the freedom which come to them on the death of their husbands, and carefully preserved by hormones, Helena Rubinstein, and hairdressers—triumphant examples of mutton dressed as lamb. It seems a pity that in America women find it so hard to grow old with grace and dignity. Nevertheless, if they keep on extending their life span, it is an art which they would do well to learn.

21

Soon after my first wife and I took up residence at Charlottenburgh, Barbara came upon a little hut not far from Charlottenburgh in which an elderly woman lived with her daughter of about nineteen and the daughter's young child, a girl. The grandmother was ill, and the little family was exceedingly poor.

Barbara picked them all up and brought them to Charlottenburgh. She took the grandmother to the hospital, where it was found that she was suffering from terminal cancer, and she died in that hospital within six months. Before she died, she asked my wife to look after the daughter and the little granddaughter, and Barbara promised her that she would.

The daughter, called Bernice, was a charming, intelligent girl and soon made herself very useful about the house. I must confess I made a few sharp objections to having her child around the place. My wife and I had never had any children of our own, and I figured that in middle life I could well do without the pitter-patter of tiny feet. So for about six months I ignored the child completely, hoping that if I didn't look she'd go away.

But she didn't go away. And, finally, I took to putting her on the seat next to me when I drove down to the farm, for she used to hang around in obvious expectation of a drive.

That did it. In no time at all I fell in love with her. I suppose my paternal glands, if there are any such things, started oozing all over the place after so many years of inaction. Her name was Veronica. She must have been about four years old at the time, an enchanting little black doll.

Barbara and I often discussed what we would do with her. It was quite a complicated problem. We couldn't legally adopt her because at that time there was no law of adoption in Jamaica. In any case, her mother lived and worked at Charlottenburgh and there could be no question, even if we had the physical means, of separating the child from her mother.

Even though there was no legal adoption in Jamaica, adoption in fact is a very common practice. In a country in which seventy-five percent of the children are illegitimate, it's a wise child that knows its own parents. Children are regularly brought up by aunts, grandmothers and other relatives. If you ask a Jamaican child the name of his parents, the chances are you'll get the reply: "I call Miss Maggie Mother." There is seldom, if ever, a mention of father. The Jamaican father is the Unknown Soldier in the battle of the sexes. He's a fast man on his feet.

Not knowing what to do, we decided to let matters slide.

We'd see that the child was properly clothed and educated and got all she needed and just leave matters where they were.

That was all right so far as it went. The trouble was that I came more and more to feel as if she *were* my adopted child. And in our district, as time went on, people regarded her as such.

In one respect, this brought out to an interesting, if distressing, degree the essential self-hate of so many black people. When Veronica got old enough to go to the local primary school, I would often have to drive her there rather than allowing her to walk, for on many occasions other black children would throw stones at her out of sheer jealousy of her position. Had she been a white child, nothing like that would have happened. Indeed, except for one or two regrettable exceptions, it was only black or "colored" people who were ever unpleasant or catty about her. There is a saying in Jamaica which well expresses this self-hate which goes: "Nayga (negroes) can't bear to see Nayga prosper."

All my adult life in public, in my columns and broadcasts, and in private when I was first so shocked on my return home from England, I had fought against the monstrous insanity of color prejudice. It was not however until I had the emotional commitment to the upbringing of a black child that I really began to learn the full nature of the problem.

I was determined that Veronica would never be touched by prejudice or, if she were, that she would be able to flick it away as she would a bothersome insect. It was easier to protect her in Jamaica. For Jamaica in 1955 had come a long way from the outpost of empire of 1935. Increasing numbers of black or colored people were in high positions of all kinds. Parties, public and private, were now happily racially mixed. Jamaica had become the most advanced country I knew when it came to racial integration. This did not mean that everything was perfect, but it did mean that the goal was in sight and we were well along the way to it.

Yet, many things still made difficulties with Veronica's upbringing. I soon found, for instance, that I was unable to find a child's book which was really suitable. Either the text or the illustrations or both showed the "heroine" as a white child, so that there was no heroine with whom she could fully identify. The same thing applied to motion pictures and even to advertisements. Such black heroes as there were tended either to be pop music stars or professional boxers. Only about three per cent of Jamaica's people were white, yet we still lived in a white man's world when it came to books, films, radio and history. The poets sang of girls with flaxen hair or with milk-white skins. Nobody sang about girls who looked like Veronica. The dream was always of a white Christmas.

Yet, it was not only the books, films, radio and history which worked to give Veronica a negative image of herself. One morning when she was about eleven and just beginning to take a solid interest in how she looked, I happened to go to her room. She was sitting in front of her dressing-table tugging at her hair with a comb and quietly weeping. I asked her what the trouble was. She said tearfully that she looked ugly because of her "bad hair."

I said, "Where have you learned that expression? Not in this house. There is no such thing as 'bad hair.' "

"Oh, yes," she replied. "There is. And I heard it here at home."

"From whom?" I asked

"From the cook. She said to me yesterday, 'What a pity! You are white people's child and yet have bad hair.' "

It took me some time to get around that business of the "bad hair." I arranged for a while for Barbara to take Veronica to her rather expensive hairdresser whenever she went and make a point of them both having their hair done at the same time, Barbara's hair being permanently waved and Veronica's being permanently straightened. Then I would complain to both that I thought women absurd, being unable to be satisfied with the kind of hair God gave them. So it was that I made the point that if Veronica's hair was "bad" because it needed to be straightened, then Barbara's hair was equally "bad" because it needed to be curled.

Just before I sent Veronica off at the age of fourteen to boarding school in Jamaica, I thought I'd better have a chat with her about the matter of color. I had been rather dreading this, just as others, in another age, dreaded having to talk to their children about sex. I had hardly begun when she interrupted me.

"Don't worry about this, Papa." She said. "I quite understand that there are people who will not like me because of my color. But God made us all, so those who dislike me for the skin that God gave me are insulting God, not me. That is their problem, not mine."

I breathed a sigh of relief and went on to another topic. I figured she needed no advice from me.

There was no adoption law in Jamaica until Veronica was nearly fourteen years old. At about this time Bernice, Veronica's mother, decided to go to New York, where she had a sister, to work and live.

Officially, Bernice had become our housekeeper. In fact, she had also become a member of the family. Veronica was even more so. She "belonged" to everyone. It could have been a tangled and complicated situation for a child, but it didn't seem to bother Veronica. She told somebody once that she considered herself lucky because while all the children she knew had only one mother, she had two. She was still young enough at the time not to consider that to be a double disadvantage.

So Bernice went off to New York, leaving Veronica with us.

At that point we could have legally adopted Veronica. But it seemed now rather pointless. She had become known as our daughter, and the formality of adoption would have added nothing. So we just left matters as they were except that I changed her surname to Cargill by deed.

Veronica was much attached to me, and I adored her. I spent as much time as I could on her upbringing, and I taught her as best I could to be utterly sure of herself, and just a little bit arrogant in a ladylike and aristocratic kind of way. As soon as she was old enough, I sent her to stay for a while with friends in England. When she passed that test, I sent her to America. She never, in either country, suffered any kind of slight; possibly because she never expected any. Indeed, wherever she went people were helpful to her.

On one occasion I had sent her to spend a week at a very well-known hotel in Miami—where at that time the color situation was not all that good. She ended up by being given the keys to the pantry by the hotel manager so that she could get herself a snack whenever she came in late. As usual, she spent all her allowance shopping and ended up broke, so the hotel manager and his wife drove her to the airport and paid her excess baggage for her, which naturally I refunded with a letter of thanks in due course.

It helped, of course, that she grew into a tall, beautiful woman, but I don't think it was altogether that.

Eventually, she met an Englishman, a chartered accountant by the name of Tom MacDonald, and married him. Had I combed the world, I could not have found a more delightful son-in-law. She was married from our house in Kingston. Just before she drove away, she wept and so did I. It was not only Veronica who drove away, it was nearly eighteen years of my life. I did not realize until she left to live abroad how much of my life and thoughts she had filled, and how empty I would feel without her. Nor did I realize my marriage would soon be at an end; or that with Veronica gone I would come to feel that there was no longer a purpose to it.

I remarried in 1975. My wife Pat is a Jamaican, like my first wife, but black. This caused a ruffling of feathers in certain quarters. I have lost no real friends because of this. It did stimulate the hostility of three Whites whom I had regarded as friends, who ceased to have anything to do with me. But that, I suppose, was all to the good. It was one way of weeding out the fair-weather sailors.

There were the usual rumblings of discontent from older Whites such as remained embalmed in my Uncle Sidney's era, and the usual backbiting from a few colored acquaintances. There is a story in Jamaica, probably apocryphal, of the well-educated colored man who goes to a public meeting and denounces the Whites and their prejudiced attitude to the Blacks. When he gets home, he discovers that his fair-skinned daughter is about to marry a black man, and he throws her out of the house.

Pat came to live at Charlottenburgh and soon settled down well with everyone, though the adjustments she had to make must have been considerable. My mother, then in her eighty-eighth year, took to Pat immediately, and that was a blessing.

I had set about in 1974 converting Charlottenburgh from a banana plantation into the growing of coconuts, as bananas were no longer profitable. Of course, as on most banana plantations in Jamaica, there were quite a number of coconut trees. But they were rapidly dying from a virus disease called, "lethal yellowing," which seems about to wipe out every coconut tree in Jamaica of the old variety. A dwarf coconut has proven highly resistant to lethal yellowing and is now being planted. I put in 20,000 of these as fast as I could. Though these trees will show some bearing within three or four years, it will be six years before they bear commercially, and I am faced with a long, hard pull.

Shortly after this my old enemy, the income tax commissioner, raised his ugly head. The government imposed penal income tax rates upon an already high rate, and this has made all private farm development impossible. The reason for this is that it is now impossible to pay off substantial capital borrowings out of earnings; there are not enough earnings left over after tax. Moreover, the current interest rate on borrowed money is 12% and it isn't possible to get a long-term loan.

So I have decided that the only thing to do would be to try to finance the development as I go along. I borrowed about half the amount that I needed and thought that I might just manage it with very considerable sacrifice.

But as I write, I wonder whether the sacrifice will not be in vain. Our problem in Jamaica is not only a political one. Is it also a problem in bad administration. The government in power is of unexampled incompetence. And as it digs our financial grave deeper and deeper, it will drag everyone down with it—rich and poor alike—with the inevitable result that the one-party state now already accomplished in practice will at last become institutionalized as the Constitution is amended to turn our monarchical system of parliamentary democracy into a republic. Why fight on in a country in which the government intends, sooner or later, to own all the means of production as well as all the minds of its citizens? I don't mind particularly risking my life, but I refuse to risk it to no purpose.

As I write this my farm manager comes in to say that all our water has been locked off. As I owe no money for water rates, this astonishes me.

"I don't know why," he says, "the man just came up and locked off the water. They even broke the pipeline and wrenched off the meter."

I have two water supplies to Charlottenburgh. One goes to my workers' cottages half a mile from my house, where it is metered. The other supply goes to another meter for domestic use in my house. The farm manager was talking about the workers' supply.

I call Claudius.

"Claudius," I say, "go down the drive to our meter there and see whether our water supply is connected."

Claudius comes back in a moment. "It is cut off, too, Boss."

I telephone the man at the parish council.

"It has been reported to me that you have been using the water supply to wash bananas," he says.

"That is not true. I could not—even if I wished. It is not connected to my banana boxing plant."

"Well, that is the report," he says. "Besides, you have not paid your bill."

"I don't give a damn about the report. And I have no bill. I want the water reconnected."

"I cannot do that without authority. I suggest you write to me and complain."

I hang up.

My farm manager says, "It's all a put-up job. I know the man they sent to disconnect the pipes. He says it is spite."

I tell the farm manager to use our own supply until I can get some sense out of the Parish Council. And I phone my lawyer, Sydney Phillips, for an appointment. Then the phone rings.

"Did you listen to the radio this morning?" my caller asks.

"No, why?"

"Well, your name was being bandied about. A report said that your water has been cut off because you are a delinquent customer. The counselor in charge of the Water Committee is quoted as saying that a wicked capitalist oppressor like you is not to be allowed to use water to irrigate your bananas."

So that was it. A set hand. I know that I am going to be in for a long battle. What the wretched counselors do not know, of course, is that I have a better private water supply than they are able to give me.

22

What with the general election, my five columns a week and all the usual problems of the plantation piling up upon me, I haven't been able to do much else for the past six weeks. The general election was by far the roughest we've ever had. Armed men held up some polling stations, substituting forged votes for the genuine ones. The police, as usual, saw only what their masters wanted them to see.

A week before the elections a young man who lives down the road came to see me. His uncle used to work for me, and I've known the young man since he was a baby. He had been distributing leaflets for the Jamaica Labour Party. A few days previously, he told me, two gunmen had come to his house. They had pointed their guns at him and told him that if he did any more work for the JLP they would kill him.

He recognized the men. They were fairly well-known in the area as henchmen for the PNP. Moreover, they drove a yellow station wagon, and the young man had taken its registration number. He went to the police and made a report. The police have done nothing in spite of the fact that the two men were to be seen driving their station wagon past the police station in Highgate almost every day.

I took the young man with me to see one of the officers in charge of the area and demanded that something be done. I was met with every kind of polite evasion. There are always dozens of reasons the police can give for not arresting anyone. Promises were made to look into the matter, but I left feeling that nothing would be done.

Two days later the young man's mother came to me in great distress. The police had arrested her son, and he was now in the Highgate lockup and bail had been refused. He had been charged with taking part in some crime or another.

There isn't, fortunately, anywhere in Jamaica that I haven't a few reliable friends to keep me informed. I have them in most government departments, in the Army and in the police. I haven't been a columnist for twenty-five years for nothing. So I went and had a very private chat with a certain Sergeant of Police.

He said, "You know why they arrested young Lindsay don't you?"

"No, I don't. But I suppose someone must have laid some lying charge against him."

"It's worse than that. The police concocted the whole thing as a revenge against him for coming to you about those gunmen in the station wagon. They don't want to be forced into having to pick them up."

"What I'm going to do, then, is kick up a fuss and threaten the police with *habeas corpus*."

"You do just that," the Sergeant said. "They have no evidence. They are bound to give in."

So I went to the police station where young Lindsay was locked up and made a very considerable scene. The next day the young man was quietly released. No charges were pressed against him. No action was ever taken against the gunmen either.

The news is not good. The State of Emergency, in effect martial law, is to continue. The bottling up of all money in Jamaica is now complete. We are allowed only fifty dollars a year in foreign currency. So even a short holiday abroad is no longer possible. Our letters are opened and read by the authorities–especially letters to and from abroad. The government agencies are bugging telephones, making tapes of conversations on the overseas lines. Bank accounts are no longer private. And for the third time last week, I have been threatened with prosecution for being critical of the government in my column.

I still can't get my water supply restored. My lawyer tells me that the parish council can be forced by legal action to restore it, but that the process will take months. The shutting off of the water is not causing me any inconvenience, but it's the principle of the thing that annoys me. The courts, thank goodness, are still intact. But I wonder for how long they will remain so.

The younger journalists and clerical staff at *The Gleaner* joined a trade union which is now demanding that *The Gleaner* fire writers like myself and replace us by people committed to the policies of this government. In the meantime, as inflation increases and firms go out of business, unemployment and poverty are increasing rapidly. Where will it all end?

Today I feel depressed. Not only because my life in

Jamaica and on my beloved Charlottenburgh may be coming to an end, but because of what is happening to the people of Jamaica.

They have had a sad history. The ancestors of 96 percent of our people were brought here by the slave ships under conditions of barbaric brutality. Sold to the slave owners on the plantations, they were regarded as chattels. Their actual conditions of work were not always as bad as they have subsequently been painted. But the great wound, exceeding any wound which could be inflicted by the whip, was to their self-esteem.

It was not a wound which was healed by the political act of freeing them from slavery. It could have done so if the nature of the cure had been understood. But it was not. In any event, our people faced, as legally free men, the same contempt and indifference they had suffered as slaves, with the added insult that they were, as free men, no longer of value. At least as chattels they had had a money value to their owners.

I do not believe that slavery from the physical point of view was any more brutal an experience than was the common lot of the English worker or the Russian serf of the same period. Jamaicans tend to place far too great an emphasis on the physical conditions of slavery, viewing it as an isolated instance instead of as part of a whole pattern. Indeed it can he said with truth that the Jamaican slave was physically better off than many of the European working classes of the time.

However, there was another dimension to the problem—a factor which did not apply to the European working class and which made special difficulties for the freed slaves. This was the matter of color and the assumption that the black person was not fully human.

It is true that the occasional English nobleman would have his butler drop his trousers before his guests after dinner in order to settle an argument as to whether the working classes had vestigial tails. Yet, as the European lower classes fought their way upwards, they had to contend with questions of degree only and not of kind.

In Jamaica, as in other similar places, the black man was indelibly marked as different in kind. His black skin was a proof of his fundamental racial inferiority. The white upper classes had on the whole no expectation that he could ever be anything else but inferior. Such was the cultural dominance of the white man's world that the black man came to share the same opinion.

Of course, he did not wholly share it. Half of him did, and half of him didn't. There was and is an ambivalence in his relationships with white men and with other black men which can be most puzzling. A black man who at one time used to work on Charlottenburgh was discussing with me some years ago the reluctance of the banks at that time to employ black tellers. He was most indignant. His well-educated daughter had applied and been turned down because of her color. Then we passed on to other topics. He told me that he was saving up to buy a radio and could he give me some money each week to keep for him. I asked him why he didn't ask the headman to do that for him. "Me, sir," he exclaimed, "me not trusting no nayger with my money."

The half of the Jamaican black man that does not share the low opinion of his own color is always understandably eager to hear opinions which will release him from the condemnation of inferiority. The other half makes him prone to mistrust his own judgment. So he tends to withhold appreciation of anything unless someone else, preferably from abroad, makes the judgment for him first.

Peculiar consequences stem from this ambivalence. One is an enormous capacity to be fooled by demagogues who know consciously or unconsciously how to play upon it to their own advantage. It saddens me to think how many times the hopes of Jamaicans have been shattered. There was the hope of personal freedom which resulted only in a century of grinding poverty. What was worse, it was not even freedom, for no man can be a "damned nigger" and yet be free.

In 1962 came another fruitless freedom called independence. There is nothing at all wrong with independence, of course, any more than there is anything wrong with a process called "freeing the slaves." But both are concepts, and unless the concept can be turned into a reality, it is a hypocritical waste of time, and independence was no more a reality than freedom from slavery.

We seem to think in Jamaica that we can alter something by changing its name. The colonial system held us in thrall for centuries, but the only escape from it for the people whose self-respect had been so monstrously savaged was to pursue two aims simultaneously, aims solidly based upon universal adult suffrage and a democratic system of government.

One was to break down the prejudice against Blacks, not by generating hatreds which as always would be self-defeating, but by applying constant pressures so that more and more significant jobs and positions would become open to them, and equipping them with the education to take advantage of these positions. This process would eventually make it no longer inevitable that people would equate a black skin with working-class status. And with the social barrier steadily disappearing, intermarriageability would emerge. As George Bernard Shaw once observed, the real solution to color prejudice is to be found in bed.

The other was to concentrate upon the creation of wealth; for in a poor country in which half of the population is under twenty, there can be no opening up of opportunities without this. Without the creation of wealth and opportunity, all that increased education can do is to educate people into unemployment and bitterness.

Manipulated by the slave traders and slave owners, given false hope by "freedom," their self-respect all but destroyed, and desperately poor for three centuries, the unfortunate people of Jamaica are urgently in need of wise and expert leadership. Instead of contributing to the support of England, our people are contributing to the support of a new elite and their thirst for power. Once again, as they have been for three centuries, our good people have been betrayed.

23

Today I have asked myself, as I have done so many times, what I can do to help. I am not a politician. For some years I have been warning the country in my *Gleaner* column, with no very great success. Yet, what more can a writer do than to write, and what happens if the time comes when I can't even do that?

It may well be that things will just putter along as they are, in which case the result will be a descent into an increasingly sordid and ramshackle poverty with ever-increasing violent crime. I want no part of that.

What really frightens me is that I can see no sensible

alternative to our present predicament. I have never run away from a fight; it would not too much bother me in spite of threats and carefully organized spite to sit it out here if there were something worth striving for. But what am I to strive for? An uprising? That will come when the people are hungry enough, but I will not fight for that; nor will I fight for another totalitarianism which could be its consequence.

Besides, there are a few domestic matters to be considered. Where can I send my stepchildren to school? I cannot send them anywhere abroad because I am not permitted the foreign currency. I would not dream of sending them to school here now that the schools no longer attempt to educate. Up to recently the problem was solved by my sending them to a school run by well-qualified American missionaries who gave their services more or less on a voluntary basis. But three months ago these missionaries felt that they should close the school and leave. I have arranged for two charming girls, teachers at one of the government schools, to give our two little girls private lessons in the afternoon after school ends for the day. They take it in turns, but can only manage an hour or two every day and that is not really satisfactory.

If I detach myself from my own problems, it is not difficult to see a long, unbroken historic connection between the sins of slavery and racialism and the tragedy of today's Jamaica. To come nearer in time, all Jamaicans including myself are suffering the consequences of all the Uncle Sidneys who ever lived—of the people who regarded blacks as nonpersons—and the consequences, too, of self-hatred and the concomitant hunger for significance which has led our people down blind alleys, following demagogues who sing so sweetly but perform with such incompetence and lust for power.

But where does that get any of us? Because a ship with a large hole in the bottom is probably bound to sink, it does not mean that one must stand on the bridge, upper lip stiff, and sink with it. That may be a grand gesture, but it seems to me that rats who leave sinking ships have a lot more common sense than the gallant captains who go down with them.

Yet I cannot contemplate leaving my home and my country without a deep sadness. For over three hundred years my family on both sides have lived and died in Jamaica. That the Jamaica of my childhood was anomalous and had to go, did not make the parting at that time any the less easy. And when in a new situation I recaptured part of it on Charlottenburgh, not by inheritance but by my own risk-taking and hard work, the idea of giving it up once again is even more difficult.

24

During the fifties and sixties, a large number of famous and interesting people used to come to Jamaica every year. Many of them came to Charlottenburgh. Of some, I have special memories.

There was, of course, Noël Coward who had a house by the sea in Port Maria and another on Firefly Hill above and behind it. Noël had a special fondness for Jamaica, and when he died he was buried at Firefly Hill, and his house and land were given to the National Trust.

Noël had a well-earned reputation for his brittle and often devastating wit. What is perhaps not so well known was his remarkable kindliness. On one occasion, for example, we had a party at Charlottenburgh and one of my guests was an elderly and rather boring lady who did not fit in at all well. After Noël and his party arrived, Noël noticed the old girl sitting in a corner all by herself, looking rather lost. He almost immediately went over and sat beside her and purposely made her feel for the next fifteen minutes that she was the most interesting person in the room. He was constantly doing things like that.

Like countless other people, I had for years enjoyed Noël Coward's plays, music and personal performances. In the early fifties I deliberately avoided meeting him though he was virtually a neighbor when he was in Jamaica. This was because I had had a number of experiences meeting people whose books or music or painting I had greatly admired only to find that I couldn't stand them as human beings, and this in turn had put me off the enjoyment of their works. This is, I know, an unreasonable attitude, because, after all, a good book is a good book even if written by a madman or a first-class egomaniac. I don't suppose I would have found Vincent van Gogh a very attractive character, but this does not make the genius of his paintings any the less. Nevertheless, Noël's plays and songs had woven themselves into the fabric of my life and I didn't want to risk getting it warped.

When eventually I did meet Noël and got to know him well, I realized that in his case I had nothing to worry about. It may seem an odd thing to say, but Noël was a greater man than anything he ever wrote. He had an exceedingly well-furnished mind and a very sharp intelligence; and on top of it all, a remarkable wisdom and balance. He seems to have decided at an early age that his undoubted "talent to amuse" was all the paying customers were going to be allowed to see of him.

Quite often when Noël felt in the mood, he would sit relaxed, looking slit-eyed and oriental, and tell us of his experiences or comment on people and current affairs. I used to wish that his commentaries could be put on tape and turned into a book. On a few occasions, I asked him why he did not write the kind of challenging and brilliant stuff of which these conversations were made. So did Ian Fleming. He would back away immediately from the suggestion with some witticism, but on one occasion he told me that he considered his own private opinions to be private. He was, he said, an entertainer and a first-class craftsman and that is what he wished to remain, so far as the public was concerned.

I came to feel that his plays, his songs, and his performances–highly skillful and enormously entertaining though they were and are–were in a sense erected by him as barriers between himself and his public and not as windows through which he, himself, could be viewed.

He often referred, in horror, to what had happened to Oscar Wilde. I suspect that the fact of his own homosexuality had made Noël resolve never to submit himself personally, as opposed to his work, to the ordeal of public scrutiny. He carried this so far that he would never get himself into any lawsuit or situation which involved his going into court. Only once, so far as I know, did he ever break this rule, and this was at the insistence of George Bernard Shaw.

There was a tacit understanding that homosexuality was a subject we never discussed, except in a very general way. Noël used on occasion to ask me to keep an eye on his house and servants when he was not in Jamaica, and one year I became very concerned about the fact that a young man called Fred, who was Noël's butler, valet, cook and general factotum, was feeding the entire village with money which he was given to spend on the house.

When Noël was in residence, the grocery bills seemed alarmingly high. I reported my misgivings to Noël on various occasions either personally or by letter and finally I suggested to Noël that he give me permission to fire Fred if he did not wish to do this himself.

Noël paid no attention, yet he continued to grumble about the expense. One evening, after dinner at Noël's house, Blue Harbour, the subject came up. I had privately concluded that the reason why Noël would not give me permission to fire Fred was that Fred had become a good deal more than just a butler, but I was trying my best not to give Noël the impression that I thought so.

I said rather irritably, "You know, Noël, there is no point in your complaining about the expenses when you know perfectly well who is causing them and yet refuse to do anything about it."

Noël looked up with a bland expression, his eyes narrow slits, "You think I'm fucking Fred, don't you? Well why not say so, and stop beating around the bush?"

I think that I blushed. In any event we never discussed the subject of Fred again.

One of the reasons why Noël so much liked Jamaica was that everyone, the press included, conspired to give him the privacy he wanted. I was fond of Noël and see no reason even now for me to invade his privacy any further than to the small degree I have already done.

Alfred Lunt and Lynn Fontanne came to dinner at Charlottenburgh. Although well on in years, they were still an elegant and handsome couple and the easiest of guests. Only the second-rate are vain, pretentious and difficult. The Lunts immediately made themselves at home, but try as I would I could not get them to talk very much about their lives on the stage. Alfred Lunt had taken up cooking as a hobby, and it happens to be a hobby of mine, too. I wish I could report a number of scintillating stage anecdotes. Instead, we spent a lot of time discussing the best way of preparing *sole bonne femme* and that most tricky of all meat dishes, beef Stroganoff.

Ian Fleming, on the other hand, with whom I had a close

friendship, was not at all interested in cooking. The "Bond" books created the illusion that he was a great gourmet and a jet-setter. The fact is that he had no palate at all and was a bit of an ascetic.

He had bought about twenty-five acres of land in Oracabessa by the sea on the north coast, and had built upon it a large and rather ugly house. It was furnished with the minimum of taste, with pictures of horses hung on the walls and sundry shelves cluttered with the seashells he used to collect. The place was called Goldeneye (it had previously been called Rotten Egg!) and it was to Goldeneye he came each year to write his Bond books.

A meal at Goldeneye was apt to be a culinary disaster. It was not made any more bearable by the extremely hard benches upon which one had to sit at table. It was after suffering a good deal of hospitality at Ian's hands that Noël Coward presented him with the following verses:*

> Alas! I cannot adequately praise
> The dignity, the virtue and the grace
> Of this most virile and imposing place
> Wherein I passed so many airless days.
>
> Alas! Were I to write 'till crack of doom
> No typewriter, no pencil, nib, nor quill
> Could ever recapitulate the chill
> And arid vastness of the living-room.
>
> Alas! I cannot accurately find
> Words to express the hardness of the seat
> Which, when I cheerfully sat down to eat
> Seared with such cunning into my behind.

* From "Noël Coward Memorial Ode," pp. 13–14, *Ian Fleming's Jamaica*.

Alas! However much I raved and roared
No rhetoric, no witty diatribe
Could ever, even partially, describe
The impact of the spare-room bed—and board.

Alas! I am not someone who exclaims
With rapture over ancient equine prints.
Ah no, dear Ian, I can only wince
At *all* those horses framed in *all* those frames.

Alas! My sensitivity rebels,
Not at loose shutters; not at plagues of ants,
Nor other 'sub-let' bludgeonings of chance
But, at those hordes of ageing faded shells.

Alas! If only common-sense could teach
The stubborn heart to heed the crafty brain
You would, before you let your house again
Remove the barracudas from the beach.

But still my dear Commander, I admit,
No matter how I criticize and grouse,
That I was strangely happy in your house
In fact I'm very very fond of it.

Ian's guests willingly put up with it all, however, because he was the warmest and most loyal of friends and a charming and considerate man. He was the sort of man who went out of his way to be kind and helpful to people, and the public image of him—tough and ruthless—is far from the truth. I think he was probably a bit ruthless to women on occasion, but then I suppose a certain amount of that is inevitable if, like Ian, you have a woman in every port and do not intend to be captured by any of them. He was, of course, finally captured by the fascinating Lady Rothermere, but after he and

Annie were married in the church at Port Maria, I often had the feeling that their relationship was one of armed neutrality rather than marriage.

Annie was, and still is, beautiful and intelligent. She can also be exceedingly difficult. She liked to surround herself with the leaders of politics and literature–the kind of people with whom Ian did not feel at home. Ian was an intelligent man, but he was no intellectual, and conversation about the higher reaches of politics, the arts and philosophy bored him. He preferred activities like swimming and scuba-diving and drinking a good deal of scotch and soda with his friends.

I think Annie was the only woman I know who could have reduced Ian to matrimony. She told me once that when she first saw him at the office of her then husband's newspaper, she resolved there and then to divorce Rothermere and marry Ian. She certainly went to her task with a will, and every year Ian came to Jamaica, she came with him. But after the wedding, she came less often This was one of the reasons which contributed to the discomfort of Goldeneye. Ian's Jamaican housekeeper, the delightful and faithful Violet, did her best, but got little encouragement.

The grounds of Goldeneye were not well kept either. Owing to a certain circumstance, matters here were rather worse than they might have been. This circumstance arose out of Ian's close friendship with a well-known and charming Jamaican woman named Blanche Blackwell, who lived in Port Maria.

Blanche has a lovely house with a fine garden, and when Ian left for England each year, Blanche would go along to Goldeneye and try her best to keep the grounds in good shape. She would plant flowering trees and shrubs, and put in perrenials of various kinds in such garden as there was. It was an uphill battle, because Ian's one gardener was no gardener at all. His only virtue was his honesty, and it was this very virtue which defeated Blanche's efforts,

Annie knew of Ian's friendship with Blanche. Annie dislikes the entire female sex as a matter of principle, but jealousy made her hostility to Blanche something very special. She knew that neither Ian nor the gardener could recognize one end of a flowering shrub from the other, so when on one of her now-rare visits to Jamaica she saw a number of new plants happily growing, she immediately asked the gardener who had planted them. Upon being told that "Miss Blanche" had planted them, Annie grasped a cutlass and chopped them all down.

This process went on for some years, with Blanche planting away with great vigor, and Annie chopping with equal vigor on such occasions as she came to Jamaica. The battle ended in a dead heat.

Eventually, we all took action to break the tie. Blanche would plant, and report to me what she had planted. The gardener was instructed, on pain of ghastly reprisals, to tell Annie that I had done the planting. This stopped Annie from wielding the cutlass. But by the time we had devised this plan, it was too late. Ten years of growth had been lost.

25

For some time in the early sixties, various people—including British publisher Andre Deutsch—had been urging Ian to write a book about Jamaica. He finally agreed to do so, provided I wrote it with him, but the project was postponed until he could finish his thirteenth James Bond novel.

Ian at this time was not well. Moreover, the writing of a new Bond book each year had become for him a treadmill. He had begun to write them as a kind of recreation, a bit of fun to be taken not too seriously. Ian maintained that he wrote the first Bond book to take his mind off marriage; a fate which had finally caught up with him in that year. When the books suddenly became bestsellers, the insistent demand for a new one each year became a burden.

At first, he had much enjoyed the success and the writing of them. It was a standing joke between us that each year we would sit over a few drinks and devise what new and kinky sexual predicament could be invented for the current book. I once suggested that he should eventually return his heroine to the missionary position which, given the public's increasing obsession with out-of-the-way sexual gymnastics, would appear to his readers to be a brand-new perversion.

But as time went on, he came to feel trapped by the whole thing. He told me that he felt he would never finish his thirteenth Bond novel. Nevertheless, Andre Deutsch flew out from England and he, Ian and I had a meeting at Charlottenburgh and signed up to do the Jamaican book.

Ian and I discussed the project in detail. We decided that it would cover various aspects of Jamaica which had interested or attracted Ian. It would consist of a number of chapters on various subjects which we would write in collaboration, and then we would add a few chapters by carefully selected Jamaican writers on other subjects upon which we didn't feel qualified to write.

The Jamaica Tourist Board became interested in the proposed book and ordered a few thousand copies from Andre Deutsch in advance. Deutsch had, in the meantime, announced the book to the trade.

The week we were due to start the real work of writing Ian became ill and was flown back to England. He died a few months later. I never saw him again.

I considered that this was the end of the proposed book. However, the Jamaica Tourist Board and Deutsch, both heavily committed to it, persuaded me to go on with it. I had an article on Jamaica written by Ian some years previously for Cyril Connolly's *Horizon* which I had intended to update and use. I also had an introduction he had written and a list of the subjects we had intended to cover. That was all.

I got a number of local writers to contribute and, eventually, got the book put together. The subjects were well covered, and the book turned out to be an excellent introduction to Jamaica. In this respect I was pleased with it. But I was not pleased by the title. The name originally chosen had been *Ian Fleming's Jamaica*, and it was decided by the Tourist Board and the publisher to retain that title.

I could see their point. A good deal of advance publicity and sales had been made on the strength of the title and to change it would have caused assorted complications and dislocations. Nevertheless, I thought the title was misleading and unfortunate under the circumstances, but I could do nothing about it.

When Ian was alive a large assortment of interesting people used to stay at Goldeneye. On one occasion, Anthony Eden, the Prime Minister of England, was given the use of the house, and he came to Jamaica to recuperate after a disastrous operation on his gall bladder. It was just after the Suez debacle and the British Labour Party Press most unfairly made much of the accusation that the best that Anthony Eden could do during the aftermath of the crisis was to loll about on the beach at Goldeneye.

Some time after this it was announced that Hugh Gaitskell, the then leader of the Opposition Labour Party, would be paying a semiofficial visit to Jamaica. Lord Beaverbrook and the rest of the Conservative press knew that while Annie Fleming's political allegiances were strictly to the Tories, she and Hugh had been close friends for years and that sooner or later Gaitskell would go to visit Annie at Goldeneye.

The hordes of photographers and reporters assigned by Beaverbrook and the rest to cover Gaitskell's visit to Jamaica were told that they should watch diligently for this moment so that the Tory press could spread over their front pages pictures of the Labour Party leader sunning himself on the beach at Goldeneye and enjoying all the "capitalist privileges" for which Anthony Eden had been criticized.

In due course, Gaitskell arrived and was invited to stay at King's House, the residence of the governor-general. Annie Fleming came to Charlottenburgh and told Barbara and me that she wanted to get Hugh away from all the official stuff for a long weekend so that he could really see and enjoy Jamaica.

Annie had suggesed to Ian that they both take him on a tour, but Ian, who for some reason disliked Hugh, had refused. What Annie wanted to know was whether we would come along with Hugh and herself as she felt that for the two of them just to go off by themselves might create a good deal of high-powered gossip and adverse press comment.

Barbara and I agreed, but there was something that worried me. Every move Hugh made was being covered by the world's press. I was at the time in the Federal Parliament and was Deputy Leader of the Opposition, and my party was the equivalent of the English Conservative Party. I thought it might have unfortunate consequences for Hugh if the press linked us together. Besides, the problem was to get the press off our backs.

With the help of some journalist friends I had the word passed around that Hugh was coming to Charlottenburgh for the weekend. I took a gamble that the English press would, as usual, have only the vaguest notion of local politics. Although I was what in England would be called a Conservative member of Parliament, my party was called the Jamaica Labour Party so my Jamaican journalist friends put it about that nothing was more natural than for Gaitskell, the leader of the Labour Party in England, to spend a quiet weekend with the Deputy Leader of the Jamaica Labour Party in the Federal Parliament. What really happened, of course, was that Hugh Gaitskell, Annie, my wife and I took off for Port Antonio and spent a lot of time in assorted places where Hugh could enjoy the "local color" and which would not have been considered at all suitable to the leader of Her Majesty's loyal Opposition.

On the Sunday of that weekend we rafted down the Rio Grande, shooting the rapids and then stopping to swim in the deep, clear pools in between, drinking strongback soup made by the raftsman from freshly caught fish and consuming a lot of planter's punch.

Gaitskell was a delightful man, intelligent and perceptive, with a highly developed sense of humor and, certainly, no ranting Leftist. He seemed to me to be quite unlike the type which usually strives for power. He was shy, with a gentle manner.

I asked him, as we floated down the river upon the raft, why he had given himself to politics. It was a question which I was striving at that time to answer for myself. For me, politics had come to seem mostly a mixture of bullshit and boredom, and I could not understand how any honest man with a reasonably open mind could put up with it for a lifetime.

He replied, "I think that politics, like marriage, is something people should go into when they are young before they have learned the disadvantages. If a man waits until he reaches the years of discretion, I doubt whether he'd rush into either."

"You don't seem to me," I said, "to be the kind of person who is greatly interested in power. Do you really want to be Prime Minister?"

He paused for a moment, dabbling his feet in the river; then he said, "Not power. No. But I must confess that I have a craving to be Prime Minister of England. Yes, I really want to be. To be Prime Minister of England is such an immense honor." Then he paused again and after a short while he said, "What you say about politicians is at least mostly true. Everyone in politics lies to some extent. I am certainly no exception. I have had on occasion to present facts, shall I say, to the best advantage of my side. But there is, you know, a vast difference between this and those who deliberately deceive as a matter of considered policy."

He paused again and then went on: "You asked me why I want to be Prime Minister. I have a negative reason as well. I must stop that bastard Harold Wilson from becoming Prime Minister. Were he to become Prime Minister of England, he would not only sorely deceive our people, but would drag the honor of England through the mud."

While we managed to buy a weekend of peace and quiet from the foreign press by my cock-and-bull story about the Jamaica Labour Party, the assorted reporters and photographers were only temporarily fooled. They soon got wise to my little deception and were busy sharpening their knives for Hugh. When Hugh turned up at Goldeneye a few mornings later to take Annie swimming, they began to move in, and by the time he and Annie emerged a small army of representatives of the conservative press were waiting outside the gateway to Goldeneye.

Annie was furious and told Hugh to drive as fast as he could to the post office. At the post office, Annie leaped out of the car to send a cable to her old friend Lord Beaverbrook, who was in the south of France, to tell him to call off his hounds as they were making life difficult for her. While Annie was inside the post office, Hugh spied the first wave of the press approaching and for some strange reason he panicked. Abandoning Annie, he drove off at high speed. He did not know his way around and simply sped off in a direction which was to him unknown.

That morning when I got back to my house around midday, I found an agitated Barbara with a number of phone messages for me. *Time* and *Life* had been phoning, demanding to know where Hugh was. There were sundry other calls from some of the other newspapers. Finally, there had been a call from Hugh. He had left a number with an urgent message that I call him there at the earliest possible moment.

So I phoned the number. It was Johnson's Hardware Store in Port Maria, twelve miles away. I asked if Mr. Hugh Gaitskell was there. The man said, "You mean de strange Englishman who is hiding behind de keg of nails?"

I agreed that it must be.

It was. And when Hugh came to the phone I said nervously, "What the hell goes on?" For one horrible moment I wondered whether he was being pursued by an angry Ian Fleming.

"Look, Morris," said Hugh, "I haven't time now to explain except to say that the press came after me and I fled. I didn't know where I was driving. After an hour I ended up here. Hiding. Come down immediately, please, and rescue me. You must do a 'Scarlet Pimpernel' act."

It seemed strange that so sophisticated and able a man should act in so childish a way, but what was done was done, so off I raced in my station wagon to rescue Hugh from behind the keg of nails. As we approached Goldeneye, I told Hugh to lie down in the back of the station wagon. He refused. He said that if the press people were waiting at the gate, they'd be bound to see him.

"I will hide here," he said. "You go and tell Annie to come and fetch me." And with that he leaped out and disappeared into the bush.

Annie was at Goldeneye. She had returned on foot from the post office. Ian had a lunch party for twelve people in progress. And Annie was at the head of the table drinking her soup. I called her out and rapidly explained the situation and sent her off. As she left, looking furious, she said, "Suppose I can't find him in the bush?"

"You will," I said, "just look for a crowd of curious children. He will be totally surrounded by now."

I went in and quietly took Annie's place at lunch. I was exceedingly hungry.

Ian was, of course, eaten up with curiosity, I kept getting imploring glances from him from the other end of the table which I ignored. After lunch Ian cornered me.

"Now," he said, "please tell me what the hell goes on? Why has Annie disappeared?"

"She's gone," I said, "to rescue the Leader of the Opposition."

"You mean Hugh? Talk, man."

So I told him what had happened.

"Silly, bloody ass," said Ian. "Good story though. I now direct that as my correspondent in the West Indies you cable the story to the *Sunday Times*."

"I will not," I said.

"I will pay you five hundred guineas for it."

"You only want to spite Hugh and the Labour Party."

"Well, what's wrong with that?"

"Nothing." I said. "But I won't file the story all the same. It might make Hugh look ridiculous."

"And why should he not look ridicuolus?"

"Because we have to stop Harold Wilson becoming Prime Minister."

"Oh, so now you're playing God. Anyway, don't swallow everything Hugh tells you. Write the story."

"I will not," I answered.

"Very well then, you bastard, come and have a brandy with me. I haven't had a chat with you in ages."

A week later, just before Hugh Gaitskell left Jamaica to return to England, he telephoned me from Kings House.

"I want to say how immensely grateful I am to you. Remember our conversation on the raft? I think I have it all wrapped up now. By 1965 the Labour Party will be in power and with luck I shall be Prime Minister. Come to visit me then and I will show you what a red carpet laid all the way to London from the airport looks like."

I never had the chance to see that red carpet. In January 1963, Hugh Gaitskell, at the height of his power in the Labour party, died. On October the Sixteenth, Nineteen Sixty-five, Harold Wilson became Prime Minister of England.

Goldeneye, when I last saw it, was growing up in bush and the house was going to ruin. Ian and Annie had one child, a son called Casper, born soon after their marriage, and Goldeneye was left by Ian in trust for him, at the age of twenty-one.

Casper was an unfortunate child. He was thrown out of Eton, his father's school, and seems to have been most unstable. He came once to Jamaica for a brief visit to Goldeneye, which ended when he attempted to drown himself. Back in England, he tried suicide again, this time successfully.

I do not know what is to happen to Goldeneye. I suppose it will be sold, if anyone can be found to buy it. The beach is uncared for and untidy, and the furniture is crumbling. The desk at which Ian sat to write the books which brought in millions is falling to pieces. Annie refuses to come to Jamaica. The faithful Violet, when I last went, was still there, still sad that her beloved "Commander" will never come back.

One more deserted house. One more ghost of the past.

26

Today being Sunday, I am summoned to an arbitration. The Jamaican peasant is among the most litigious of people, chiefly, I think, because the courts of law were among the few places in which he was treated as an equal. The Jamaican will spend an immense amount of money on lawyers' fees to settle the most trivial issues.

I have not for years been in the active practice of law except for a brief few months some time ago when my friend Sydney Phillips was in urgent need of temporary help with his court work. He asked me if I would take his cases in the local Resident Magistrate's courts for about three months until he could complete his arrangement for a new partner in his law firm.

I had never practiced in the courts in the country parts of Jamaica and was shocked when obviously poor people came to my office and produced, in cash, ten or twenty pounds as a retainer in some matter which I was sure could be settled out of court. I tried my best to tell them this, but soon learned that what was really at stake was a question of honor.

One one occasion there was a dispute between two neighbors over a boundary line. The argument had grown heated and hard words used. Virtually the whole small district had been drawn into the dispute, and partisan feelings were running high. When the matter ended up in court, the court was packed with supporters of both parties.

After the case had been proceeding for about two hours, the judge addressed both the plaintiff and the defendant. He said, "From the evidence given up to now, it appears that you two have been neighbors and friends for years. The dispute between you seems to be relatively trivial. Why do you not just get together and shake hands and settle the matter? Why let a thing like this spoil a long friendship?"

The plaintiff looked at the defendant and the defendant looked at the plaintiff. Both moved smiling towards each other and shook hands warmly. They had a brief discussion. Then the older of the two turned to the judge.

"With respect, Your Honor, we have followed your advice. We have made friends. But now, sir, we are asking you please to continue to try the case."

Too many bets between their supporters had been made on the outcome, and too many arguments needed to be authoritatively decided for the two friends to spoil the fun by a private settlement.

Contests over relatively trivial matters are not, however, always confined to the peasantry. The very first case I handled for Sydney, I acted for Prince Ferdinand of Liechtenstein, who was also involved in a matter of honor.

Ferdinand had consulted Noël Coward about where he could get some tropical suits made, and Noël had recommended a tailor in the small town of Port Maria. Ferdinand then bought some cloth in Kingston and took the cloth to the tailor to make him two suits.

When the two suits were delivered, Ferdinand did not like them. He refused to pay the tailor, and complained to Noël. Noël was furious with Ferdinand. He told Ferdinand that he had no right to expect a West End of London quality of work, and rebuked him for his meanness in not paying the tailor. Relations between Ferdinand and Noël became strained.

Then the tailor, unable to collect, sued the Prince. This infuriated Ferdinand, who apparently considered it beneath his dignity to be sued by a tradesman. He consulted Sydney Phillips, and instructed him to defend the action, and to counterclaim against the tailor for having ruined seven yards of good cloth.

I came on the legal scene just the day before the claim and counterclaim were due to be heard in court, and Sydney asked me to appear for the Prince.

On the day of the hearing before Mr. Justice Nash in Port Maria, the courthouse was packed. This absurd confrontation had, by this time, inflated itself into a *cause célèbre* between Noël's friends on one side, and Ferdinand's friends on the other. It had reached the point where celebrities, local and international, were cutting each other dead at cocktail parties. Both sides, including two dukes, an earl, a number of knights and assorted theatrical notables of both sexes, were well represented among the spectators at court. All it needed was a bishop or two to make Port Maria look, that morning, like a chessboard.

English law does not require that a person who is making

or repairing something show any greater skill than what in normal circumstances could be reasonably be expected of him. If you give your watch to a motor mechanic to repair, you cannot complain if he does not exercise the skill of an experienced Swiss watchmaker. A small tailor in a small West Indian town would not normally be expected to exercise the skill of Savile Row. The prince's case depended, therefore, upon how badly the suits had been made, and how expert the tailor could be said to have held himself out to be. I had to establish two major points if I hoped to win. The first was that the tailor had held himself out as capable of the best and most sophisticated quality of tailoring. The second was that the suits, when completed, were well below this standard.

I banked on the tailor's vanity and craving for self-advertisement before such a fashionable gathering to undo him on the first point. Under cross-examination I asked him, "Sir, are you trying to tell the court this morning that you are capable of making a suit fit for a prince?"

The tailor, bridling, puffed his chest out and answered. "Sir, I have made suits for many celebrities, including Mr. Noël Coward, and they have all been pleased. Indeed, sir, I am capable of making a suit fit for a king!"

He got a round of applause. He was delighted. So was I.

The second point needed more attention. I spent quite a lot of time trying to establish that the suits were ill-fitting and poorly cut, but the test would come, of course, when finally I put my client into one of them to prove my contention. Having come to the case at the last moment, I had not had the time to look at the suits. I had simply been going on my client's statement that the tailor had not made them properly. Before the court rose that day, it was decided that on the following morning the judge's chambers would be made available for Ferdinand, where he would change into one of the suits for a personal appearance in court.

I told Ferdinand that he would have to bring the suits to court without fail.

"I cannot," he said.

"What do you mean, you cannot?" I said impatiently. "Our case depends on it."

"I forgot to tell you," Ferdinand said with downcast eyes, "but I was so fed up with the suits that I gave them away to my gardener-boy."

"This is one hell of a time to tell me that!" I said angrily. "You will just have to get them back from him, that's all. Otherwise, I wash my hands of the case."

The following morning, upon my arrival at court, Ferdinand was there, looking very pleased with himself, grasping a large brown paper parcel.

"I was in luck." He said. "I got the suits. Here they are."

"Don't give them to me now," I said. "There isn't time. Let's go to the judge's chambers right away."

I left Ferdinand in the judge's chambers to change into one of the suits, and went upstairs into the courtroom.

In due course, Ferdinand entered the packed and expectant courthouse. He was an astonishing sight. The jacket was halfway down to his knees. The trousers were narrow around the ankles with wide turn-ups. The pockets were stitched around with colored thread. It was what was then known as a "zoot suit," of the kind one would expect to see on a pimp in Harlem.

There was a hushed silence in court for a moment, and then laughter broke out. I noticed that Ferdinand was signalling to me and trying to say something, but I indicated to him to be quiet and to go into the witness box. It gave me pleasure to notice that the lawyer for the tailor was standing with his mouth half-opened in horror.

When Ferdinand got to the witness box, I rose and said, "May it please Your Honor. My case rests." And I sat down.

The judge then looked at my opponent's lawyer and asked him if he had any questions.

"No, Your Honor," he said, wiping his forehead.

My client got judgment on both the claim and the counterclaim, with full costs. It had cost the poor tailor a packet.

As we were walking out of court, I said to my client, "Ferdinand. I had no idea the suits were all that awful."

"They were not," Ferdinand said.

"What on earth do you mean?"

"Well, that was what I was trying to tell you in court, but you wouldn't let me."

"I don't understand."

"It's like this," Ferdinand said. "As I told you, I'd given the suits to my gardener-boy. When I got them back from him this morning before court, they were all wrapped up and I never saw them until I was putting on one of them in the judge's chambers. The boy had obviously had them altered to his style. They were quite nice suits when the tailor sent them to me. Not like this at all."

"Great God!" I said, horrified. "We shall have to go to see the judge. I can't be a party to misleading the court."

We went to Mr. Justice Nash in the lunch hour in his chambers. He was very nice about the whole thing.

"You did your duty, Morris," he said, "by bringing this matter to my attention, and I believe your client when he said he had no intention of misleading the court. In any event, the attorney on the other side was a fool. He should have asked your client in court whether the suit he had on was in the same condition as when the tailor delivered it. The truthful answer to that would have helped us to elucidate the matter. He is a good lawyer. I think he must have been temporarily paralyzed at the sight of your client." The judge chuckled.

"What are we to do now?" I asked.

Ferdinand butted in. "I hold nothing against the tailor,

except that he should not have sued me. I had to teach him a lesson."

"I cannot reverse my judgment now," the judge said, rubbing his brown bald head with his hands. "But suppose," he added, peering at Ferdinand through his horn-rimmed spectacles, "I were to get the tailor in here to see us. Could there not be a quite unofficial adjustment?"

"I would be glad to cooperate," said Ferdinand.

He was an honest man, and now that his wretched honor had been successfully defended, he clearly had no wish to be spiteful.

A constable was called, and the tailor and his attorney were summoned. Fortunately, they had still been in the environs of the courthouse. They entered the judge's chambers, looking puzzled.

Ferdinand was most generous. He explained at rather inordinate length that he had been defending his honor, but that now that there had been a judgment in his favor he was prepared to pay for the suits and for all the tailor's legal costs. He produced the money in cash. He had, in any event, a rich and open-handed American wife. The tailor was delighted. The tailor's attorney was delighted. Mr. Justice Nash was delighted. We all shook hands with everyone else and left in a warm, self-righteous glow.

Two weeks later Noël Coward came to dinner and took me to task for appearing for Ferdinand.

"How could you," he said, "have appeared for that mean bastard Ferdinand and been a party to bullying my poor little Port Maria tailor? I'm ashamed of you."

I was stung into self-defense. I told Noël about what had happened and how Ferdinand had paid all the tailor's legal costs in cash, amounting to a very considerable sum.

"Say that again," said Noël. "Do I understand you to say that the tailor had all his costs paid by Ferdinand?"

"Exactly and precisely," I said.

"Goddamn that tailor!" cried Noël, slapping his forehead. "Would you believe that I guaranteed his costs and yesterday he collected all the money from me?"

"Serves you right," I said.

As I started out to say, I am summoned to an arbitration this morning. This is an arbitration on my farm and has nothing to do with the courts. Every now and then my workers get into some kind of argument, and they ask me to come along and settle it for them.

Today's problem seems as if it may be a bit complicated. When I get to the large empty garage, I find that a table and a chair have been set up for me. About fourteen people are there and my farm manager steps up to the table after I am seated. The rest of the people cluster around.

"We are asking you today to settle something, Boss. It is a matter between Ramjus, Mrs. Ramjus, and Rachel. You know Rachel who works in the boxing plant."

"What's the problem?" I asked.

"Last month, Rachel have a baby. Rachel is going along with One-Seed. One-Seed say the baby not his."

At this point, Rachel pushes to the front of the group. She is carrying a baby in her arms. She turns to the others and says, "You don't say nothin' more. I will ask Boss the question."

She came up to the table, opposite to where I sit. "You look at dis baby, Boss," she says.

I get up and take a look. The baby certainly does not belong to One-Seed. It is a pretty little thing, half Indian, with a fair skin. Both Rachel and One-Seed are black.

I say, "If you want me to tell you who exactly the father is, that is not possible. But I can tell you that the father is Indian, not black."

"You think him coulda white?" asks old Miss Clementina who is always teasing me. This gets a laugh.

"Thank you, Boss," says Rachel.

A tall black fellow steps forward. He says, "I want to tell you who de father is."

"How can you know?" I ask. "By the way," I add, "What is your real name, One-Seed?"

"Paul, Boss."

Why do people call you One-Seed?"

"I lose one testicle in a railway accident."

The second ranger, a thick-set brown-skinned man called Cripple because he has a slight limp, pushes forward and says, "He have two children by Rachel, Boss. The one seed he have can do the work of two."

"Who is the father of the child according to you?" I address this question to Rachel.

"It is Ramjus, Boss."

"Do you agree with that?" I ask One-Seed.

"Yes, Boss."

I think it is about time that the man accused of being the father has his say. So I ask Ramjus what he has to say about it.

"I must be the father, if you say the child is a half-Indian, Sahib."

I am now thoroughly puzzled, for there seems to be no disagreement about the paternity of the child.

"Well," I say, "there seems to be no doubt as to who the father of the child is. What is the trouble?"

Mrs. Ramjus steps forward. She says, "I am a legally married woman. My husband's child belongs in my home. I want de child."

Rachel intervenes with indignation. "It is my child, Boss. I not giving up de child. It is de first lookable child I have. Look at his good hair, Boss." She pushes the baby forward, "Look how his skin fair. I not giving him up."

One-Seed interrupts. He says, "Mrs. Ramjus have no right to de child. Ramjus is not a good man."

I am now more puzzled than ever, for everyone seems to be taking the "wrong" side. I say to One-Seed, "Listen to me,

One-Seed. Are you vexed because Rachel had this child by Ramjus?"

"It don't go like that, Boss. Rachel is a good woman. I have two child by her. She look after me well. We have to sport sometimes, you know, Boss."

The ranger, Cripple, interrupts. "Cho. Stop all that, man. Boss know all about sport."

"Him sport too much," Miss Clementina interjects. "You can't tell Boss 'bout sport."

There is considerable laughter all round at that. I feel matters are getting out of hand. I say, firmly, "Now stop your joking. Mrs. Ramjus can't have the child. The natural guardian of a child is its mother, and Rachel loves the child. Am I right, One-Seed, is saying that you don't mind if Rachel keeps the child?"

"She *must* keep the child, Boss. I give her a damn good lick already for it, but I don't vex anymore. De child is a nice child."

"Well, what in the name of God is all the argument about?" I ask. "You all seem happy, except for Mrs. Ramjus, and she wants what she can't have."

"The thing don't settle yet, Bossy," says One-Seed.

"What is not settled?"

"Ramjus, Boss. He behaving wicked."

"Well, er, yes," I say, somehow feeling that I still haven't got the point.

"Him is a mean man, Boss. It cost me forty dollars for hospital and doctor when de child born, and him refuse to give me a penny."

At last I was home and dry. I had the measure of the dispute now. I said, "Ramjus. If you knew you were the child's father and caused this expense, why did you not pay?"

Mrs. Ramjus spoke before her husband could reply. "If him to pay money, him must get de child."

"That is not how it goes at all," I said. "Ramjus you must pay One-Seed forty dollars."

"I don't have de money, Boss."

"Him damn lie," Rachel cries indignantly.

"Now listen to me, Ramjus," I say, "don't tell me any lies. I know you have forty dollars. Go and get it now, otherwise I will dock your pay."

A murmur of assent goes up from the group.

"Well, now, are you happy, One-Seed?" I ask.

"Sure, Boss."

Rachel turns to Mrs. Ramjus. "You can see the child anytime you know. He can spend day with you. I don't have nothin' against you. But Ramjus must do him duty."

So the arbitration ends, and I go back to my house. I wonder how many similar situations in Europe or America could be settled in such a civilized and rational manner, and with such regard and respect for all concerned. I wonder how I, myself, would react in similar circumstances had I been in One-Seed's position. I have the humbling suspicion that it would be me, and my kind, who would behave like "ignorant natives."

I suspect that our opinions on and attitude to practically everything are far less influenced by our intellects than we like to believe, and are to a much greater degree the products of how we live.

One of the consequences of large-scale urbanization is the wide gap which now exists between people who do things and people who mostly just think or talk about things. For instance, there was an occasion when a young couple from New York came to visit us at Charlottenburg. They arrived at about eleven in the morning, and I asked them what they would like for lunch. They said barbecued chicken. So I told

Claudius to chop the heads off a couple of chickens, pluck them, and give them to the cook.

It just so happened that as my young friends were strolling around the house, they came upon Claudius cutting off the head of the second chicken. They were horrified. Having lived all their lives in a big city, they had never seen a chicken except as a prepared, packaged and cellophaned item in a supermarket. The shock of seeing a living thing actually being killed to provide their lunch was tremendous. The young wife was in tears. The young man said that he was going to think seriously of becoming a vegetarian. I had to give them something else for lunch. I gave them steak instead, and refrained from mentioning that we had butchered the steer the week before.

Yet even those of us who have lived less artificial lives are still greatly separated from many of the realities we pontificate about. Shortly after I passed my law finals, a legal friend, thinking that I should have some exposure to the actuality of legal institutions, took me on a kind of guided tour which included St. Catherine District Prison in the old city of Spanish Town.

There, my friend and I, as a very special favor by the governor of the prison, were allowed the "privilege," as he called it, of attending a hanging.

I had spent many hours before this arguing with friends about capital punishment. Capital punishment had been an intellectual concept which one quoted statistics about or defended or attacked on principle. Today I was about to understand capital punishment as an experience of the emotions.

There was the short but solemn walk from the condemned cell to the room which housed the gallows; the priest walking alongside the condemned man, intoning prayers; the prison governor in front, and two guards bringing up the rear. Then, upon arrival, the hangman stepped forward putting the black hood over the condemned man's head, the guards guiding him directly under the rope which was now put around the man's neck, the knot just under the left ear.

At which point the condemned man started to scream in terror, crying and screaming that he did not want to die, and begging for life. The hangman jumped to his lever, and even before the priest finished his prayers, he had sprung the trap and the body dangled—silent at last. Then the hangman descended the few steps leading beneath the trap and ran his hands quickly down the body, pushing down the erection which, with the ejaculation, had been brought on as a reflex as the neck broke.

If my friend had not half-supported me, I think I would have passed out. I sat down on a wooden bench trying to pull myself together. After a short while, the governor came along with a man beside him.

"I thought you'd like to meet the hangman," he said.

The hangman was a middle-aged, well set-up, dark brown man with graying hair.

"This is my fiftieth drop," he said with pride.

"He's made his half-century today," said the governor. "And he's never had a failure yet. A wonderful record."

The hangman, a matter-of-fact, kindly-looking man, looked me up and down and then made what I suppose was his standard joke with visitors.

He said, "You wouldn't need much drop, sir. You've got a good weight for the size of your neck."

"Does the amount of drop vary?" I asked, more for something to say than for any other reason.

"That is the art of it," he replied. "The long, thin types with strong necks need a lot of drop. You gets so you can tell the drop needed at a glance. I used to have them weighed, but long time now I don't bother. Enough drop and the knot placed just right, and they don't know a thing."

It is all very well arguing about capital punishment, but hanging with all the mumbo-jumbo is something else.

What we should fairly ask ourselves is whether we, ourselves, could act as hangman. I know for certain that I could not. Perhaps it would be easier in the U.S., where one pulls a switch. In any event, what happens socially to a man who is a professional hangman? Will his friends come to dinner with him? It is considerations of this kind which become important in a world which is moving towards a universal middle-class. I am to hanging what my New York friends were to barbecued chicken.

I suspect that hanging and barbecued chicken will both eventually become things of the past, not as the result of any resolution of an intellectual issue, but because nobody will be found willing to hang a man or decapitate and pluck a chicken. Unless, of course, a computerized machine is developed to do both jobs. And in some way I find hard to explain, such a prospect seems even more frightening.

27

About three weeks ago Brother Man came to me to say he had some business to conduct in Kingston and would be away for a little while. I begged him to be careful and not to carry any ganja with him in public places.

I did not see him again until yesterday. As I drove in from Highgate, I saw him walking along the road in the direction of where I was coming from. I stopped and asked him whether he was coming back to Charlottenburgh. He said he would be later that day, but he never turned up. This did not surprise me immediately. Jamaican time is elastic. Ras Tafarian time is Einsteinian.

But as I sit in my study I hear a commotion outside, and Claudius comes running in.

He says rather breathlessly, "Brother Man come back. He can hardly walk. Somebody beat him up. He asking for you."

I go outside in a hurry. Brother Man is indeed in bad shape. He is limping painfully. He has a large bruise under his left eye, and the eye is nearly closed. He takes off his shirt and shows me that there are bruises all over his back and one on his right side over his ribs.

"What on earth has happened to you?" I ask him.

"De police, boss. De police do it."

"How?" I ask. And we help him along to a chair on the back verandah. He sits down with a grimace of pain.

"Yesterday they pick I up at Highgate. They say, 'You damn rasta bitch—what you doing here?' They take I and lock I up. And then they take I out, knock I all over with de gun butt and ask I why I come to Highgate. Dey hurt I bad. Then this morning day take I out again and I think they are going to kill I. So I tell them I work with you. When I tell them that, the Sergeant says to let I go."

"Were you charged with anything?"

"No."

I say angrily that I am going to raise hell about this, but I suggest that he goes to his cottage and lie down.

"I will drive you down," I tell him.

"No, Boss," he says and then adds surprisingly, "I not going back to no cottage."

"Why, Brother Man?" I ask. "Were you not happy here? You need time to recover."

"I very happy here with you, Boss. But Rastaman must not stay in any place too long. I stay here too long. Jah send I a sign." He points to his bruises. "Jah send I a sign to move. I too long in Babylon."

His mind is made up, and I know from experience that if

I argue with him I will only get a long spate of incoherencies.

"You and I is friends," he says. "I would like you to give I ten dollars."

"Where are you going?"

"Where Jah tells I."

"Where is your mandolin?"

"It is where it is safe."

So I give Brother Man ten dollars and hold out my hand. I have never shaken his hand before because Brother Man, like many Ras Tafarians, does not like to be touched. But he gets up and takes my hand briefly and shyly.

"Goodbye, Brother Man," I say. "I shall miss having you around."

"I will not forget you, Boss. Jah willing, I and I will meet again." And he turns about and limps away down the driveway. I do not even bother to phone the police. With Brother Man not here to give a written statement, it is a waste of time. Even with a statement it would be a waste of time. Who would accept Brother Man's word against a whole team of policemen?

28

Today I have made up my mind. An old friend from America came to me two weeks ago and said very simply, "Are you ready to go?" It was as if he had been reading my mind. It is a quality he has. I noticed it first some years ago when I was deeply troubled over my first marriage. As usual, he was there offering his immense kindliness in a way that people seldom offer help—without insistence, without even appearing to be very concerned, but simply radiating a sort of reassurance—and he seemed at that time to be a jump ahead of my own thoughts as if he read them before they had been properly formulated.

I said to him in answer to his question, "I think I would like to discuss the matter with you."

My friend has another quality which takes getting used to. He is impatient with all discussion beyond the absolute minimum. He is also irritable if he thinks he is being railroaded into the open acknowledgment of a kindly act. He said, "I don't want to discuss the matter with you. I only want to know if you are ready to go. If you are, I want you to join my business in America."

I said, "How much notice will you require?"

"Oh, two hours will do," he said with a smile.

I did manage to get him to amplify his statement a bit two days later. He spent most of the time informing me that his offer to me was entirely selfish on his part and had been stimulated solely by his own self-interest. This was not true, of course, and was designed to protect my self-respect. But I said nothing, for I knew better than to accuse him of an act of sheer friendship. No accusation would have infuriated him more.

I was deeply relieved at this offer, for without the prospect of some job in America, I could not leave Jamaica, since only fifty dollars for each adult is allowed to be taken out of the country. Many things still had to be done.

I took a deep breath and phoned the real estate firm of my old friend Bobby Alexander. Bobby was, as usual, somewhere over the Atlantic in a jumbo jet.

The general manager said, "It is almost impossible to sell a plantation these days. Who the hell wants to buy anything in Jamaica? You will have to take a very low price. About half its value—assuming it can be sold at all. But I know Bobby would want us to pull out all the stops for you so I'll put everyone on to it."

"How long do you think it will take you to sell it?" I asked.

"Oh, my God. What a question! We might both be in

our coffins before I can sell it. Or maybe in a month. I don't know, but leave it to me."

I had to accept a low price, but at least a purchaser was found. Alexander's took only two days to find him. I wouldn't be able, of course, to take out of Jamaica a penny of what was left after the mortgage was paid off, but at least I had found somebody who would keep the farm going and my workers employed for the time being.

So I have made up my mind to leave. Tomorrow the trailers will be here to take all our furniture and household articles. I hear that even taking one's personal possessions will soon be blocked so I am acting as quickly as I can.

It has been a long time in our family since we were displaced persons. On my father's side, the displacement to Jamaica was from Scotland near the end of those shameful twenty-eight years between 1660 and 1688 when monstrous crimes were committed by Scotsmen upon Scottish men and women in the name of religion.

It was just before his execution at Edinburgh on the tenth of July 1681 that Donald, my ancestor, quoted from Isaiah 26:20, "Come my people, enter thou into thy chambers and shut thy doors about thee: hide thyself as it were for a little moment until the indignation be overpassed."

For the people of goodwill who must remain in Jamaica, I cannot improve upon that advice.

I suppose I should count my blessings; we have had three centuries between moves.

Claudius comes and knocks on my door. . . .

"What is it?" I ask him.

"You know that macadamia nut tree we planted ten years ago?" he says, "It is just bearing for the first time."

"God damn that tree! Why would it have to bear now!"

I go outside and look at everything in the garden. Soon I shall not see my plants again. Or my cat which, doglike, walks along with me as I stroll through the garden. I see everything clearly and in sharp detail. I look at them intently so that they shall always live on in my memory, and I pick up my cat and hug her. She rewards me by rather painfully scratching my nose.

For two days now the phone calls, the telegrams, the letters have been pouring in. There had been rounds of lunches and dinners, formal and informal, to say farewell to Pat and me. But there is one farewell that I am dreading.

I get into my car to go see my mother at her house in Kingston for the last time. A car in front of me displays a sticker on the back which says, "Will the last person to leave Jamaica please turn off the lights."

My mother is ninety-one and unwell, but mercifully has all her wits about her, as if she were a young woman. She cannot walk easily for she has a painful arthritic hip and is sitting in her wheelchair when I arrive.

There is nothing much that I can say to her. She has had her hair done and in spite of her age is looking beautiful and aristocratic and calm. She says, "I have had my hair done so that you won't remember your mother as an ugly old woman."

I say, "I am going to miss you, Mama."

"And I you. You must write often."

"I shall see you again soon," I say, "for I shall be back for a while after I settle down."

"I am glad you are leaving Jamaica," she says. "You have made the right decision. My life is over here. And I am bored. Since your father died and Peter died and John went away, I have had only you. Jamaica is no place for either of us now, but I am too old to move. At any rate, not to another country." And she smiles.

Both my mother and I hate goodbyes.

I say, "Well, mama, I must go now." And I take her in my arms. When I let her go, she swings the wheelchair around and turns her back upon me. I turn and walk away. I know, as I turn, that I shall never see her again. I can hardly see where I am going. I get into my car and drive back to the hotel where Pat and I are staying on the day before leaving. When I get to our suite, the sitting-room is full of people. I cannot talk. I cannot even see them. I go to the bedroom and sit on the bed. I am back a lifetime to when I first said good-bye to my mother when I was leaving for Munro. But I knew then that I would see her again. Now I know that it is the final chapter. Pat comes in and puts an arm around my shoulder and knows she need not say anything. I wish I could weep, but I cannot. There is just a sense of irreparable loss. And I remember how to deal with it. I get up and go out to my guests.

POSTSCRIPT

And so Pat and I and the two little girls left Jamaica. We arrived in New York with a hundred dollars between us and were met by our friend at Kennedy. It was on February 10, 1977. The cold ate into our bones.

On the morning of July 12 my mother died. Among her papers was a letter to me to be delivered to me after her death. It was a short letter which read:

My darling Morris,
I lie awake in bed most days and nights and long for death to release me. From the day you were born I have

loved you more than anything else in the whole wide world. You have been a wonderful son to me. God bless you, my precious son, May all be well with you.

Mother

Now that my mother has died I have no longer any ties to Jamaica nor any present wish to return, but I have memories of Jamaica and her people; of her rivers and her mountains, her sunlight and her white sand. And of the handsome black faces singing of loves and hates and hopes.

Above all, I have memories of Charlottenburgh, and of the peace and beauty it brought me.

I know the ugly side of it, too. The poverty, the injustice, the prejudice which were like open wounds to our people; wounds which were beyond the power of my generation to heal; wounds which will heal themselves only with time.

I know, too, that in memory there is a kind of immortality, and that if only I can keep my memories bright and well-furbished, all the plants and creatures and people, Miss Elizabeth Selvyn, my handsome father and my beautiful mother, all whom I have so greatly loved in my time, will not for me die. The folly will pass. The beauty will remain. One day, I know, I shall return home. But, for now, I have been too long in Babylon.

Epilogue

Nearly two years after leaving home in Jamaica, my wife, the two stepchildren and I returned. My half-brother John Pringle, had flown from England to New York came to New Jersey to visit me. He made it clear that he didn't approve of my leaving Jamaica. He encouraged me to return and fight and not just run away. He told me that he was flying to Jamaica in a few days and invited me to join him.

But before writing about my return, I should tell you

about my eighteen months of exile in New Jersey. I had to make many adjustments and my first problem was to find a place to live. After much searching I found a charming block of town houses, staid and old-fashioned by American standards. These were in a town named Englewood and I was most eager to rent one of them.

The rental agent explained to me that I at no time in the history of Brinkerhof Manor had a house been rented to a family with children.

After chatting with the rental agent, she suddenly said, "Mr. Cargill, you seem like such a nice man that, despite our no children rule, I'd like you to meet Mr. Brinkerhof."

I agreed. The day before we were to meet, I had been interviewed by Barry Farber on radio station WOR. Mr. Brinkerhof happened to hear the broadcast and when we met, I found him in a most affable mood. He was a product of Harvard and a delightful and elegant man but I must confess that his views were quite right-wing and I could not imagine why he had liked so much of what I had said on the radio show. In any case we got on well and then we came to the subject of the house.

"How many children do you have, Mr. Cargill?" he asked.

"Two," I said. "And I understand you don't allow any."

He looked at me, then smiled. "Well, Mr. Cargill, there's always a first time! You can have the house."

"I am most grateful to you," I said, "but there's something else I'd better tell you. The children belong to my wife and my wife is a bit dark. In fact, she's as black as the ace of spades.".

I held my breath. I knew this was an all-white neighborhood.

Brinkerhoff stared at me again. Then, with a friendly

grin on his face he said, "Well, Mr. Cargill. Like I said, there's always a first time."

We moved in without delay, but with the nervous expectation that our greeting by the other tenants would be a flaming cross set up in the front garden.

But there was no flaming cross. Indeed the neighbors could not have been more friendly, even supplying my wife and children with sandwiches and soft drinks as we struggled to get our furniture and belongings in place.

This helpfulness and kindness to my wife and children and to me was symptomatic of our life in Englewood. The only awareness of a color problem I ever had came about in an inverted kind of way. A few days after getting my driving license and finding it difficult to drive on, what to me was the wrong side of the street, I was driving my children to school and promptly turned onto an avenue on the wrong side. Flustered, I went through a red light and then, even more flustered, I turned the wrong way down a one-way street. Having got myself disentangled to the sound of terrible oaths from sundry drivers, I proceeded on to school in Englewood only to have a very angry cop in a police car signal me to stop.

The police officer got out of his car and coming across to me said, "What the hell do you think you are doing? I'm going to throw the book at you." He was a black policeman.

I was trying to mollify the cop by explaining to him that I was a foreigner and not used to driving on the right side of the road, my two little girls got out of the car to walk the rest of the way to school. The cop looked up and saw them.

He said "Are those children yours?"

When I said yes his anger seemed to vanish. He smiled at me and exclaimed "Soul brother! Go your way in peace, man! Go your way in peace."

And with that he got back into his police car and drove off, leaving me to wonder at the strange ways of the country that was now my home.

There were other difficulties. In order to settle into our new house we needed a number of things, so I went to a large shop in Englewood and bought a refrigerator, a television set and a number of other costly items. The proprietor with whom I was dealing asked me for my credit card. I didn't have one. A few days previously having been told that in America one should have a credit card I went to my bank to get one. The bank manager told me that I must give him a list of the shops with whom I had credit transactions so that my credit-worthiness could be gauged. I explained to him that I had been brought up in a very old-fashioned way. "I have never," I said "in all my life ever bought anything on credit or on installments."

The bank manager looked at me in a strange way. I think he thought that I was trying to hide something.

"Well," he said brusquely "I am sorry but we can't give you a credit card."

I've never been able to understand why a lifetime's habit of paying cash is so damaging to one's credit in America.

So I had to tell the proprietor that I had no credit card and no hope of getting one. But I offered to pay by check.

In England or in most British countries, when you give a check in payment, the recipient can phone the bank and receive confirmation that your bank balance will cover the amount. I discovered with some dismay this cannot be done in America.

"You know," I said to the proprietor, "why don't you accept my check and trust me? I have never passed a rubber check in my life."

"How do I know that?" he said.

I remembered Mr. Binkerhof's words and repeated them: "There's always a first time."

He took my check and of course it was good. Then, in some strange way word seemed to spread around Englewood that there was an eccentric Limey in town who didn't have a credit card and who paid by check. Apparently it was decided to humor me. In any case I never afterwards had any problems paying by checks. I gave my checks to supermarkets, drug stores, dry cleaners, garages and so on and was never refused.

Even stranger, perhaps, was the small but pleasant matter of the attendant at the entrance of the New Jersey Turnpike. My wife, I regret to say, had discovered that a Jamaican ten cent piece, which was worth nothing, was the same size and weight as an American quarter so she got into the habit of paying her way on the turnpike by casting these worthless coins in the basket. The toll the light would turn green and say "Thank you!" without sarcasm.

Then every time she stopped the car to enter the turnpike an attendant would give her a little present such as a stick of chewing gum, or a piece of chocolate or perhaps a candy. He never forgot to do this. As a result my wife gave up paying in worthless coins and used proper American quarters saying that the attendant's kindness made her feel ashamed.

I often wondered whether he knew exactly what she'd been doing and had decided to improve her morals by kindness.

When I told my friends about the attendant and his little gifts and about my checks being accepted and about my neighbors feeding sandwiches to a black woman and her two children, and about the cop who called me soul brother, they didn't believe me and probably don't to this day.

Nevertheless during all my time in America I never received anything but kindness and decency from everyone with whom I came in contact. My eighteen months sojourn in Englewood was one of the happiest periods of my life.

With my half-brother's visit this period was soon to come to an end. I left my wife and children in New Jersey and flew down to Jamaica with John. This book is not about politics but some mention of politics is necessary.

Jamaica was still suffering greatly from a socialist regime imposed on it by the People's National Party and Michael Manley, its leader. It was not so much the socialist ideology which was causing the trouble but the sheer incompetence of the government. Out tourist trade had been ruined, capital investment had dried up and there was a serious flight of capital. In the markets, there were severe shortages of goods of all kinds. In one sense, however, there was one good sign. When the P.N.P. had come to power in 1972 it enjoyed immense support from the masses but in the eighteen months I had been away, the people became disillusioned.

I told my half-brother John that he was correct and it was my duty to return to Jamaica and help to fight for a change of government.

We also discovered, almost by accident, that a beautiful 800 acre farm in Portland called Paradise was for sale. John asked me to have a look at it and when I reported to him that it was a lovely place, he did something typically generous with his usual speed. He bought it. Then he said whether I liked it or not he was giving me a half interest in it in return for running it and that I should remain in Jamaica and develop it properly. I returned to Jamaica with my wife and children.

The farm needed attention. It had fine land and a river

running through it. We borrowed a good deal of money from the bank and I set to work.

I also set to work to help organize the parish for the next General Election which was to be held in 1980. In that year there was almost civil war and politics took the lives of 800 people.

In the General Election held in 1980 the P.N.P. was swept out of power in a landslide victory for the J.L.P. and the nightmare era of the 1970's came to an end.

However, Jamaica had other troubles. For 150 years, the Jamaican people used marijuana as a social lubricant. Its use never escalated to hard drugs and any problems it caused were minor.

For twenty years I had been advocating in my columns and broadcasts that it should be legalized, for it had become illegal during the 1920's at the urging of the British government. But the law was very loosely applied and ganja, the local weed, continued to be widely used without much incident.

Alas, during the 80's, America suffered one of its Puritanism attacks and started a war against its use. The American experience of Prohibition, which created the Mafia, should have warned them that the prohibition of marijuana would create a similar disaster.

Jamaica was dragged into this war and the first thing that happened, of course, was that the street price of marijuana shot up sky high. The high price stimulated the growth of smuggling and gangsterism. Soon the gangs which had taken over the trade in marijuana found that cocaine and heroin, being much less bulky, were easier additions to their trade.

This time there was no Mafia but a pest of Jamaican gangsterism just as bad. These gangs are well known as posses in the U.S.A. or as Yardies in England and are giving our country a very bad reputation. It is wonderful how often those who seek to do good trail evil in their wake.

When the Jamaica Labor Party came to power led by Edward Seaga, Michael Manley went into the political wilderness. When the political tide turned once again some years later, the P.N.P. came back to power led again by Michael Manley. But during his years in the wilderness he had abandoned his socialism and had become a born-again advocate of private enterprise. No more now of politics except to say that the P.N.P. which is currently in power under a different Prime Minister, is administering a capitalist regime with the same incompetence it brought to socialism.

During 1980 there was a very serious hurricane and the developments I had instituted at Paradise, every field which had been planted, was blown flat. In any case my eyesight was deteriorating. John and I decided with heavy hearts that we had had enough of agriculture and we sold Paradise.

I now occupy my life solely with writing and reading, and live in Kingston where this end piece is being written.

Jamaica continues to be the most beautiful island in the world in spite of the current epidemic of hooligans and crime. I count a large number of Jamaicans as being splendid and charming people and hope that the unfortunate phase that we are now going through will pass.

In any case I will never leave Jamaica again. For good or ill, Jamaica is my homeland and has been the home of my family for three centuries. As I am now an older man, I have no doubt that a departure from this earth is not very far away. But this time, it will not be exile to a foreign country unless the Elysian Fields can be so described. I would be quite content if such a destination turned out to be at least as pleasant as Englewood.